MEVLANA
CELALEDDIN RUM
AND
THE WHIRLING DERV

Third published in 2005

ISBN 975-7499-09-9

Publishers
Dost Yayınları San ve Tic Ltd. Şti.
General Yazgan Sok No:13/3
80050 Beyoğlu / İstanbul

Tel: (212) 245 31 41 - Fax: (212) 245 75 83

www.dost.ws

ACKNOWLEDGEMENT

The publisher wishes to thank the following for aid in securing the transparencies of illustrations: Nurhan Atasoy, Filiz Çağman, Zeren Tanındı. He is also indebted to Mrs Ingred Iren for kindly reading the galley proofs and making valuable observations.

Photographs By Ara Güler, Haluk Konyalı, Mustafa Türkyılmaz and Basın Yayın Genel Müdürlü

Color Separations By Ebru Grafik

Printed By Seçil Ofset

Talat Sait Halman/Metin And

Mevlana Celaleddin Rumi and The Whirling Dervishes

Sufi Philosophy - Whirling Rituals
Poems of Ecstasy - Miniature Paintings

Art Editor: Salim Şengil

A Dost Publication

Contents

The English versions of Mevlana's poems are by Talat Sait Halman unless otherwise credited. Many of the poems are quoted partially.

The initials TSM, used in identifying the source of some of the illustrations, stand for Topkapı Sarayı Müzesi, The Topkapı Palace Museum.

FOREWORD

"The day will come," Mevlana Celaleddin Rumi said to his son Sultan Veled according to a 14th-Century source, "When Konya will flourish and our tomb will rise in the center of the city. Arriving wave upon wave, multitudes will visit our mausoleum and will always speak our words." Those who visit the Central Anatolian city of Konya will bear testimony to the accuracy of the prediction made by the great mystic philosopher and poet whose followers, the Mevlevis (known in the West as "The Whirling Dervishes") kept his ideas, verses and rituals alive for more than seven centuries. Particularly from December 2nd to 17th every year, when many thousands from all over the world congregate in Konya to commemorate the anniversary of Mevlana's passing in 1273 from worldly life to his soul's union with his Beloved God, his Sufi ideals and humanistic teachings find a new efflorescence. The city that Mevlana called "The Mecca of the Heart" resounds with his dithyrambic poetry and the ritual whirlings of his followers who seek communion with God through love, music, and graceful, mesmerizing turns.

Mevlana is a cultural figure of world stature who gave not only Turkey and the other Moslem countries but people everywhere the transcendent values of "the heart's purity," the images of the Perfect Man, the deathlessness of the loving soul, joys of passion, humanitarian enlightenment, the artistic dimensions of faith, and the poetic euphoria of the belief in God's beauty and in the human being as a reflection of that reality. He sought to create a "climate of love" when sectarian conflict was rampant and religious wars ablaze. Few faiths in history have shared Mevlana's total commitment to peace or his insistence on blending ethics with aesthetics.

This book is an attempt to provide an explanation of the symbolic meanings of the Mevlevi whirling rituals and to offer insights into the ideas and ideals of Sufi thought. Prof. Metin And's article is a detailed account of the ceremonies of the dervishes and the focal significance of music and dance as an act of mystical faith. My article deals with Mevlana's concepts of love, ethics, art, humanism, universalism and God the Beloved. It is based on extensive quotations from his vast corpus of exquisite and exuberant poetry. The book is embellished by splendid miniature paintings relating to Mevlana and the Whirling Dervishes.

It has been a pleasure to collaborate on this book with Prof. Metin And, one of my close friends, who enjoys international fame as a leading scholar of the dramatic and other performing arts. Mr. Salim Şengil, a well-known Turkish short story writer and one of Turkey's most enlightened publishers, conceived of the idea of producing this book. Metin And and I are grateful to him for his interest and meticulous care.

Our thanks are also due Dr. Jayne Warner who gave the manuscript a thorough reading and made many extremely valuable suggestions concerning its substance and style.

It is our hope that this book will provide to its readers insights into the philosophy and poetry of Mevlana, one of history's greatest mystics, and into the symbolism of the dervish rituals. We also hope that the readers will gain an appreciation of the eminent poet-philosopher's civic consciousness and his total faith in God without the stringencies of organized religion.

The words of praise Mustafa Kemal Pasha (Atatürk), the founder and first president of the Turkish Republic, wrote in the Visitors Book of the Mevlana Mausoleum during his visit to Konya in 1924, stand as a most eloquent tribute to Mevlana Celaleddin Rumi:

"Every visitor to Mevlana's Mausoleum is a refugee from reactionary dogma...The idea of soaring to God standing, whirling, in motion is a natural expression of the Turkish genius...Mevlana is a lover of transformation who transcends the ages, a great reformer who welded Islam to the Turkish soul... Mevlana upheld the principles of social revolution and the freedom of conscience."

Talat Sait Halman

NOTE ON SPELLING

This book employs standard Turkish spelling for most of the proper names and special terms. Some of these appear in other publications in a wide variety of versions. A typical example is Mevlana's name. Its most common modern Turkish transliteration is Mevlana Celaleddin Rumi. But Mevlana appears in many English-language publications as Mawlana, or Maulana, often with macrons over the second and third a. The variations of Celaleddin are Celâleddin, Celalüddin, Jalal al-Din, Jalal ud-Din, Djalal al-Din, etc., also with occasional macrons or circumflexes.

Terms which have entered standard English vocabulary, e.g., dervish, appear here in their Anglicized forms.

For many names and titles in Arabic or Persian, the most common transliterations in English are employed.

The pronunciation of Mevlana's full name in Turkish may be phonetically shown as follows:

Mev - lah - nah
Dje - lah - led - dean
Roo - mee

The following is a simple guide to modern Turkish spelling and pronunciation:

a (like *gun*) var. â (like *are*)
b (as in English)
c (like *jade*)
ç (*ch* of *chin*)
d (as in English)
e (like *pen*)
f (as in English)
g (*g* of *good*)
ğ (makes a preceding vowel longer)
h (*h* of *half*)
ı (like the second vowel of *portable*)
i (like *it*) *var.* î (like *eat*)
j (like *measure*)
k (*k* of king)
l (as in English)
m (as in English)

n	(as in English)	
o	(like *eau* in French)	
ö	(like *bird* or French *deux*)	
p	(as in English)	
r	(*r* of *rust)*	
s	(*s* of *sun)*	
ş	(*sh* of *shine)*	
t	(as in English)	
u	(like *pull)*	var. û (like *pool)*
ü	(like *tu* in French)	
v	(as in English)	
y	(*y* of *you)*	
z	(as in English)	

Of the twenty-nine characters in the Turkish alphabet, six do not exist in English: ç, ğ, ı, ö, ş, ü. The letters q, w, x are not in the Turkish alphabet although they may occur in foreign names. The letter ğ has its own capital, Ğ, but never starts a word. The undotted ı and the dotted i are separate vowels whose distinctions are strictly observed in pronunciation and spelling. These two letters have their individual capitals as well: I and İ respectively.

LOVE IS ALL:
MEVLANA'S
POETRY AND PHILOSOPHY

by Talat Sait Halman

(Above) The historian Mustafa Ali presenting his work to Mustafa Pasha: *(below)* Whirling Dervishes in their ritual dance. *(TSM H. 1365)*

What is this whirling of ours?
A greeting from the inmost friends of the heart.
When their messages arrive
They give the weary soul vigor and comfort.

Caught in this wind, the mind's branches
Reach out and bloom all over again.
One gentle flap
And the body finds its peace.

The rooster crows at dawn
In the climate of the soul:
The sentinel's cry
Resounds with the King's triumph.

At the roll of drums,
The ecstatic soul
Pulls out a fistful of arrows
And takes aim at the body.

A strange sweetness, never felt before,
Spreads through the flesh,
And the mouth revels in the luscious taste
Of the reed flute and the player's lips.

Look at these thousands of scorpions
Writhing, curling, dying...
We hold no drink in our hands,
Yet the hour of a thousand joys whirls around us.

This is the festivity where amulets are made
Against the scorpion's sting;
The sorcerers who fight the scorpions
Live in the disrrict of love.

From all sides
The hesitant Jacob springs to his feet
When he catches from far away
The smell of Joseph's coat.

Mevlana Celaleddin Rumi encounters his consecrator Şemsüddin of Tabriz (TSM H. 1230)

All creatures were born
At the flourish of the trumpet;
The dead shall wake and rise
In adoration of that flourish.

Those who are frozen forever
Unmindful of this music
Those who are lower than the dead
Shall now turn into the quintessence of dust.

The body that absorbs this blessed wine
And the heart that gets drunk on it
Have been roasted in the fire of longing--
Now they are ready to be devoured.

Words can never contain or portray
Or praise the beauty of the invisible face;
Look deep with a thousand borrowed eyes
It still lies beyond sight.

G. Scotin maj. sculp.

There is such a Moon in your heart
That even the sun in the sky
Keeps declaring:
"I am your obedient servant, your slave."

Be like Moses,
Look into that Moon in your own heart:
To find your joy and bliss
Look through your own window.

Let the whirling run wild and take flight
Never mind what the blockheads say;
For you are life added to the life of whirling ecstasy,
You are the glittering joy of the age.

With his poetic celebrations of love and the arts and life itself, Mevlana Celaleddin Rumi heralded in the 13th Century a new glittering age of humanistic mysticism. His ideas which stressed the deathlessness of the loving soul, the joys of passion, the inherent worth of the human being, the aesthetic as well as the ecstatic imperative of faith, the need to go beyond the confines of scholasticism and to transcend schisms, and above all the Godliness of Man not only gave renewed vigor to Islamic mysticism but also represented for the Islamic religion in general a counterpart of the Renaissance which was to emerge in Europe a century after Mevlana's death.

Recognition of Mevlana's enduring moral force in the Islamic world and his intellectual impact elsewhere has prompted many prominent figures to praise him. Hegel saw him as one of the great poets and thinkers in world history. The British Orientalist Reynold A. Nicholson, an indefatigable translator of Mevlana's verse, paid tribute to him as "the greatest mystical poet of any age." For his *Westöstlicher Divan,* Goethe drew inspiration from some of Mevlana's poems translated into German. One of the immortals of Persian classical poetry, Jami (d. 1492), said of him: "He is not a Prophet, but he has written a Holy Book," referring to the *Mesnevi* (Persian original: Mathnawi), which has also been called "The Koran of Mysticism" and "The Inner Truth of the Koran." Rembrandt drew him from a miniature painting. Sir Muhammad Iqbal, the national poet of Pakistan, proclaimed: "Mevlana turned the soil into nectar... I became drunk on his wine; now I live with his blessed breath." Iqbal once advised his son: "Choose Mevlana as your guide so that God will grant you love and ardor." Gandhi used to quote his couplet "To unite —that is why we came / To divide, that is not our aim." UNESCO's first Director-General, Julian Huxley, lauded his spirit of international brotherhood. In 1958, Pope John XXIII wrote a special message: "In the name of the Catholic world, I bow with respect before the memory of Mevlana."

Jalal al-Din (Celaleddin) was born in Balkh (in present-day Afghanistan) in 1207, the son of a renowned scholar and mystic, Bahaüddin, who was forced to flee from Balkh with his family when Celaleddin was about 12 years old. The reason has not been fully documented, but it was probably either an impending Mongol onslaught or an intellectual-political disagreement with the Sultan and his entourage. The family wandered through Persia and the Arab lands for ten years without finding a city receptive to Bahaüddin's independent spirit and unorthodox ideas. Finally Konya welcomed them.

Konya (ancient Iconium), which St. Paul had visited three times, had been a Seljuk city for nearly 150 years. The capital of the Turkish Seljuk Empire, it was ensconced in high culture and enjoyed a climate of tolerance and freedom. Although predominantly Turkish and Moslem, the new home of Bahaüddin and his family had a cosmopolitan population with Christian, Jewish, Greek and Armenian communities. Islamic sects and non-Moslem communities coexisted and flourished. In his introduction to the *Discourses* of Mevlana, the British Orientalist A. J. Arberry observes:

> Where was any country to be found in which true believers still dwelt, uncontaminated by the blight of heresy and fanaticism, under the protection of a just and religious king? In every place Daya asked this question, and always he was given the same answer — in Rum, those provinces of what is now Asiatic Turkey which were still ruled over by the western branch of the once immensely powerful Saljuk House.

The Seljuk Sultan Alaeddin Keykubat, according to legend, sent Bahaüddin an exceptionally strong invitation pledging that, if the great scholar and his family would settle in the Seljuk capital, the Sultan "although he bows to no one is ready to become Bahaüddin's faithful servant and disciple." Legend also has it that, when Bahaüddin, having accepted the invitation, was arriving with his family and retinue, Sultan Alaeddin met them outside the city, dismounted, and walked to the distinguished scholar who remained on his horse. The Sultan wanted to kiss Bahaüddin's hand, but Bahaüddin held out his sceptre, the symbol of his moral authority, which the Sultan respectfully kissed. Then the Sultan held the bridle of the scholar's horse and, remaining on foot, led the way. That is how they entered the city of Konya, the Sultan paying homage in public to the higher spiritual and intellectual authority. Until Bahaüddin's death, the Sultan regularly attended his sermons and lectures. In the words of Sultan Veled, Mevlana's son: "The Sultan and his commanders faithfully visited him / And wholeheartedly ate the honey of his counsel."

Celaleddin was 22 years old when he arrived in Konya. He lived there until his death on December 17th, 1273 at the age of 66. The city afforded for him the atmosphere and the opportunity to evolve and express his new ideas which received cultural values from the diverse religions and sects active in the Seljuk capital. He achieved distinction as a young theologian and Sufi (mystic). It was in Konya that his philosophy engendered the Mevlevi movement or sect (which has come to be known in the West as "The Whirling Dervishes"). Mevlana's ideas and ideals of spiritual purity, love and understanding, the aesthetic dimensions of faith, humanism, intellectual freedom, and universalism found fertile ground and took root in the heartland of Anatolia.

In 1244, a dramatic encounter changed Mevlana's spiritual life. In Konya he met a wild mystic who seemed to have come out of nowhere — Şemsüddin of Tabriz. Their meeting has been referred to as *merc ül bahreyn* (convergence of the two seas). It is said that Mevlana discovered the inner secrets of love through the influence of Şems — and came to the realization that love transcends the mind. At this stage in his life, at age 37, he was above all a scholar. He had read in depth in Persian, Arabic, Turkish, Greek, and Hebrew, and commanded vast encyclopaedic knowledge. But now passion reigned supreme over his mind. The frontiers of the intellect suddenly appeared too narrow, constricting, claustrophobic.

As a result of his affection, perhaps love, for Şems he embarked on a period of virtually constant ecstasy and excitement, of poetic creativity, of immersion in music — and the *sema*, mystic whirling. Symbolically, he became a torch that Şems fired. Their friendship has been likened by the French author Maurice Barrès to that between Socrates and Plato or between Goethe and Schiller.

Şems, a compelling figure of mysterious power, put Mevlana through many rigorous, and occasionally cruel, tests from which Mevlana emerged obedient, selfless, deepened and enlightened. Şems seemed to answer Celaleddin's prayers for *pathei mathos*:

I yearn for a lover who wreaks havoc by rampages,
Whose heart burns, who drinks and spills blood, defies the stars, wages
War against Heaven, whose fire — even when it takes a plunge
Into the bottom of the vast sea — still flames and rages.

The symbolic acts of Şems could be quite bewildering. According to legend, proclaiming that "the science of love cannot be mastered in a religious school," Şems decided to forbid Mevlana to read books, including his own father's writings. One day, sitting by the pond, Şems dropped Mevlana's books one by one into the water while Mevlana looked on without complaint, perhaps acquiescing in the belief that the true mystic must divest himself of all conventional learning. It is said that it was Şems who prevailed on Mevlana to start and stress the *sema* as an artistic means of experiencing ecstasy and achieving mystical communion with God, the Beloved.

After fifteen months of friendship during which Mevlana was in bondage to his moral and mystical guide Şems (whose name means "Sun" — the sun that enlightened Mevlana) mysteriously disappeared. Mevlana was shattered, in deep despair: "Without his face, Paradise for me is hateful Hell." He composed heart-rending poems full of images of burning from separation, of unbearable longing, of spiritual exile: "Come, come, in your absence, I have lost my mind and my faith."

This sequence of events was, in fact, a perfect mystic phenomenon. For Mevlana, Şems constituted the embodiment of God as well as the symbol of humanity. He, in effect, found God and became part of the Godhead. The disappearance of Şems had its correlative in God's abandoning mankind. In Şems's absence, Mevlana was to undertake an arduous mystical search. He went to Tabriz and Damascus, but failed to find the Sun of Tabriz. When he finally received word that Şems had been seen in Damascus, he sent letters in verse: "O the light of my heart, come back! O my lover and loved one, our life is in your hands. Come, I pray." Şems did not reply — like God who does not answer the prayers of the mystic. Finally Mevlana's son, Sultan Veled, and other disciples went to Damascus and brought Şems back to Konya. Mevlana's beloved Şems, whom he called "the flying sun," was back: symbolically Mevlana had found God again, this time to merge his soul utterly and inseparably.

The voice of love is descending from left and right:
We are bound for Paradise. Join us. Watch this sight.

We were in Heaven - - the seraphim know us well,
And now we must return to eternity to dwell.

Between all this dust and pure life lies an abyss - -
We fell. Let's hasten back to the homeland we miss.

He wrote a poetic celebration of reunion:

Blessed moment. Here we sit in this palace of love, you and I.
We have two shapes, two bodies, but a single soul, you and I.

The colors of the gardens and the songs of the birds
Among the flower-beds will make us immortal, you and I.

The stars of heaven will come out to gaze at us - -
We shall show the stars the moon herself, you and I.

United in ecstasy, we shall no longer be you or I.
Rescued from foolish babble, we shall rejoice, you and I.

All the bright-plumed birds of Paradise will plunge into grief
When they hear us laughing merrily, you and I.

A few months after the reunion Şems was gone again. It was rumored that a band of assassins, jealous of his closeness to Mevlana, murdered him for "political" reasons.[1] Mevlana refused to believe that Şems had died. "How," he asked, "could the sun die?"

He lives the eternal life, yet "He is dead!" says someone.
He is the sun of hope. Who can claim death for such a sun?
It is an enemy of the sun who climbs on the roof,
Covers both his eyes and shouts: "Look, the sun is dead and gone!"

It is said that the whirling dance, to the accompaniment of the reed flute, is an expression of the lament for the absence of Şems — the death of the human God. It was after this momentous event that Mevlana went in search of his true God, the God in the outermost reaches of his own soul.

The passions of the mystic mind which Mevlana called "my spiritual kingdom," intensified by his pains and ecstasies, gave rise to his collection of odes and quatrains entitled *Divan-e Shams-e Tabriz* and the complete lyrics embodied in *Divan-e Kabir* in Persian.[2] In many poems, the poet identifies himself with Şems, using the Sun as his pen name. Most of those fervid lyrical verses, composed in strict classical forms and meters, were extemporized by Mevlana while in a state of trance, his soul enraptured, bursting out into effusive euphony. It was reported by his contemporaries that "there was a pillar in his house, and when he drowned in the ocean of love, he used to take hold of that pillar and set himself revolving around it. Meanwhile, he versified and dictated, and others wrote down the verses." The great *Mesnevi*, consisting of some 26,000 couplets, was also dictated in more or less the same fashion to Mevlana's friend and disciple Hüsameddin. Sometimes they would spend entire nights, Mevlana dictating and Hüsameddin writing at a furious pace, chanting it all as he transcribed. Virtually all of Mevlana's poetry was reportedly composed this way, or while doing the *sema*, as an amanuensis called *kâtib ül-asrar* (scribe of secrets) took it down.

It is small wonder that the great mystic was given the supreme title of Mevlana (Persian: Mawlana, meaning Our Lord, Grand Master). His reputation rests not only on the spiritual heights he attained in his poetry, but also on having brought the dimension of aesthetics to mysticism in a systematic and comprehensive way. Poetry, music, dance, and the visual arts — rare in most Islamic movements — were integrally combined in the practices of the Mevlevi Order. Not only the synesthesia of the verbal, musical, and visual genres, but more comprehensively, the unified use of intellectual, spiritual and artistic elements constituted the hallmark of Mevlana's faith.

Mevlana may well be the only major philosopher in history to express and formulate an entire system of thought in poetic form. This assessment is not merely a converse of Coleridge's statement in *Biographia Literaria*: "No man was ever yet a great poet without at the same time being a profound philosopher." Taken together, the *Mesnevi* and the *Divan-ı Kebir* represent perhaps the world's most resourceful synthesis of poetry and philosophy, embracing the lyric, narrative, epic, didactic, epigrammatic, satiric, and elegiac norms. Two other comparable achievements come to mind: *De Rerum Natura* by Lucretius and the *Divinia Commedia* by Dante. Mevlana's poetry is superior to *De Rerum Natura,* and his philosophy is, in many respects, more effectively articulated in substance and structure than the *Divinia Commedia.* In a way, the *Mesnevi* is a forerunner of Dante's work. Dante's own description of *Divinia Commedia* is essentially applicable to the *Mesnevi*: "The poem belongs to a moral or ethical branch of philosophy, its quality is not speculative but practical, and its ultimate end is to lead into the state of felicity those now enduring the miserable life of man." Significantly, the norms of humanism which characterize the work of both poets appeared first in the Moslem mystic: at Mevlana's death, Dante was only eight years old. Petrarch came a full century later, and Erasmus lived two and a half centuries later. Mevlana's *Divan-ı Şems-i Tebriz* could be considered the first major "sonnet sequence" in world literature, antedating both Petrarch and Shakespeare.[3]

Mevlana's poetry is a vast geography over which many seasons range and change. It embodies the aesthetics of ethics and metaphysics. His *Mesnevi* makes a monumental synthesis of mystic ideas ranging from Neo-Platonism to Chinese thought, embracing Indian, Persian and Greek mythology, stories from the Holy Books, Arab and Persian legends and folk stories; it provides for a schema or even a system of philosophy, insights into psychology and the laws of physics and logic, *lumina ingeni.* Regrettably, many scholars have denuded or numbed Mevlana's poetry while trying to explain his philosophy. Yet, unlike most of the works of ancient philosophy, including those of the Moslem mystics, Mevlana's works are stimulating reading. As Hegel writes at the end of his *Encyclopaedia,* in exploring God as absolute mind, "if we want to see the consciousness of the One... in its finest purity and sublimity," we cannot do better than to read Mevlana's verses. There is always an excitement, a revelation, passions raging or exquisitely controlled, a symmetry of ecstasy, an order of divine madness. Mevlana achieved, as Homer had done, the ultimate, the near-perfect work of his own genre. Certainly, no mystic poet has surpassed him in the seven centuries since his death.

The academy of Mevlana, not unlike Aristotle's Lyceum, was a sanctuary for humanism where a whole spectrum of ideas was discussed freely, with tolerance, without malice. In it, souls capable of creative surges experienced ecstasy. There, art was Godliness, poetry the word of love and faith, dance the circle of joy. Mevlana was obviously right when he said about himself:

The whole wide world has yet to see
The wine that moves me to ecstasy.

He took pride in the new dimensions of mysticism he introduced:

The vendors of old goods are gone. We are
The new vendors, this is our bazaar.

He viewed conventional religious tenets and institutions as restrictions on intellectual independence and the freedom of conscience. For him, orthodoxy was inimical to true faith. He denounced it in vehement terms in a *rubai*:

Unless the seminaries and the minarets perish,
The wandering dervish can reach no state he can cherish.
Unless faith becomes disbelief and disbelief is faith,
No vassal of God will be a true Moslem and flourish.

A scene from Mevlevi whirling

He stressed the supremacy of love over formal religion:

Only fools praise and glorify the mosque
While they oppress hearts full of love and faith.

— — —

Beyond belief and faithlessness there lies the space
In whose heartland this love of ours has found its place:
It holds no room for religion and sacrilege - -
That's the ground where the man of wisdom rubs his face.

The conventions of religion, according to Mevlana, inflicted pain on the people:

The holy month: The people are bewildered and in pain.
Why beat the drums? You can see it with your own eyes, it's plain.

The drums make all that clamor - - like the outcry of evil.
The Lord is deaf, that's why the drums blast again and again.

No poetry is more sorrowful than mystic poetry about spiritual exile, about the agony of separation from God the Beloved. But, in Mevlana's vision, there is no place for the abysmal fallacy which, in the dogma, segregates God and man:

At one time when life was real, your soul was one with my soul:
All we were, open or secret, was part of the same whole.
If "you" and "I" are pronouns I use, they are only terms - -
In truth, there can be no separate you or I at all.

His monistic Sufism holds that man is not only God's creation, but also God's reflection. There is no duality in the universe. There is oneness, unity. The enlightened individual, the person who loves is part of God.

The mystic predicament is that he or she has fallen apart from God's

reality and beauty temporarily. The divine image, God's human manifestation, yearns to return to the beloved Godhead. The mystic feels a sublime love which remains unrequited until he suffers so intensely in his spiritual exile that he finally reaches a blissful state of the submergence of his selfhood, the death of his ego.

The Sufi search for God has three stages: purification, enlightenment, and union. He must abandon all physical appetites, guide himself to the elevation that love makes possible, and finally merge his soul into God's reality. Mevlana distilled this progress into just a few words:

Since we have passed
The night of the flesh at last,
We are ourselves the Guide
And life's immortal tide.
(Tr. A. J. Arberry)

The time of attainment is celebrated in one of Mevlana's most rhapsodical *rubais*:

This is such a day: the sun is dazzling twice as before - -
A day beyond all days, unlike all others - - say no more...
Lovers, I have great news for you: From the heavens above
This day of love brings songs and flowers in a downpour.

The arrival, this spiritual triumph, gives the mystic soul God-like powers:

Such is my life, though I came into the world yesterday,
Today I have built anew this whole crumbling world.

After the long, arduous search for God ends, the mystic has the strength to destroy temporal political power:

I drip out of a spout drop by drop - -
But like the deluge I crush myriad palaces.

The Sufi spirit triumphs in giving joy, in creativity:

We have a soul that creates so many joys,
If the world crumbles we would build a new one.

According to Sufism, true love renders life supreme, victorious over crass existence, transcending the confines of material life. Mevlana's vision affirms that *omnia vincit amor,* "love conquers all." One of his *rubais* declares:

As salt resolved in the ocean
I was swallowed in God's sea,
Past faith, past unbelieving,
Past doubt, past certainty.

Suddenly in my bosom
A star shone clear and bright;
All the suns of heaven
Vanished in that star's light.
(Tr. A. J. Arberry)

Mevlana promised ultimate uplifting happiness to the acolytes:

Whoever joins the circles of our faith to go our way
Sees that in our body hundreds of lives have their heyday;
Whoever drinks nectar from the pitcher of our spirit
Finds such blissful ecstasy that he takes our night for day.

The mystical experience includes not merely a temporary loss of the sense of time but also, far more dramatically, an all-encompassing awareness of all ages of man, of transcendent and triumphant time:

To become a mystic, feel no longing for the past. Gage
The affairs of bygone days - - and you shall turn a new page;
You shall then be the child of the time, its youth, its old sage,
And never lose the hour you are in, the core of the age.

The night of whirling leads to the highest truth, to an experience of divine wisdom:

Tonight is such a night - - the core of the darkest layers;
Tonight is such a night when answers are found for prayers - -
The night of gifts, grants, and offerings, the night of bounty.
Such a night: we share the secrets of God like soothsayers.

Mystic anguish nurtures and validates faith and optimism, because it is bound to create its own imitations of Paradise:

Even if the world is covered with thorns all over
The lover's heart is still a rose-garden.

Love leads the Sufi to the spring of Godly life. Mevlana beckoned that spring, that terrestrial and celestial Paradise, in beautiful words:

Dark is the flesh, as raven's wing,
And cold the world as wintry day:
Darkness and cold! But come, spring,
And drive these sadnesses away.
(Tr. A. J. Arberry)

The Sufi hopes and prays that everyone will share in the joys of love:

Let each soul find a ladder up to the skies of joy,
Let no one's back be arched like the sky because of sorrow.

One of his most subtle *rubai*s evokes the mystery of spiritual elevation beyond the proverbial spring. But only a unique soul is capable of it — a single branch among all the trees:

This season is not the spring, it is some other season,
The languid trances in the eyes have a different reason,
And there is another cause for the way each single branch
Dallies by itself while all the trees sway in unison.

And there is nothing like the exuberance of the mystic:

Perfect, perfect, perfect
This love is three times perfect;
Empty, empty, empty
This flesh and its lusts.

Sacred, sacred, sacred
This light is three times sacred;
Soaring, soaring, soaring
To meet eternity today.
(Tr. A. J. Arberry)

Mevlana celebrated love in a poem which certainly ranks as one of the best paeans to love in any language:

This is Love: to fly heavenward,
To rend, every instant, a hundred veils.
The first moment, to renounce life;
The last step, to fare without feet.
To regard this world as invisible,
Not to see what appears to one's self.
"O heart," I said, "may it bless thee
To have entered the circle of lovers,
To look beyond the range of the eye,
To penetrate the windings of the bosom!"
(Tr. R. A. Nicholson)

In Mevlana's vision, the depth of the heart is God. Reason is pitiful compared with love: "The madman of love is above all reason," and "The thrones of the Sultans, pitted against love, are pieces of wood." In purifying himself, the mystic divests himself of earthly appetites: "The road is far from lust to love."

One of his quatrains expresses the outburst of love out of tranquility:

Every night flowers blossom in the sky,
The universe is at peace, so am I.
Then hundreds of sighs break out in my heart
Where in cold darkness flames rise with each sigh.

Love is the antithesis or even the negation of despair and death:

Old Winter's reign of Death is undone,
Regret is dead; Love lives again.

The mystic, often called a heretic and a sinner by the zealots, is willing to yield to the temptation of love:

I took a vow that so long as life does not fade away
From my heart, I shall stay on the straight path and never stray;
But then I looked to my right and to my left - - and I saw
My beloved right and left - - left and right - - every which way.

One of his striking poems blends the human and metaphysical dimensions of love:

Why does the heart rage with flames in the dead dark of the night?
I thought I saw the dawn, but what has become of daylight?

The eyes of love are huge, no day or night can contain them...
My love's eyes have covered all eyes, leaving them without sight.

Love's quintessential glory found eloquent expression in Mevlana's lines:

Love is the Sultan of Sultans: Both worlds bow at his feet.

— — —

In the sect of love, there is neither faith nor sacrilege.

— — —

Love has no body, no mind, no heart, no soul.

— — —

Love lies out of the reach of dogma.

— — —

The light that reason sheds is a false dawn.
Dawn's real beauty can be seen not by the eye, but by the heart.

Love, according to Mevlana, gives the mystic access to all time and space: "I am a drop that is both a drop and the vast sea." He proudly asserts about love:

Its glory in my soul
Is as a sea profound
And in that sea is all
The world of Being drowned.
(Tr. A. J. Arberry)

In a superb quatrain, he posited love as all-embracing, and his friend — reference to both a beloved human and God — as absolute bliss:

So long as I am alive, love enlivens each day.
I am not a hunter, but this is my cherished prey.
This is my moment, my epoch, my stand through time,
My heart's calm, my peace, my friend who ends all dismay.

Mevlana conceived of love as the be-all and the end-all, complete in itself, absolute in value:

Love needs only Love to declare itself
As the sun needs just the sun to bare itself.

For him, love is the paramount component of mystic theology:

The religion of love is apart from all religions;
The lovers of God have no religion but God alone.

Mevlana's aspiration was to remain outside of, and to transcend, national and religious schisms. The spiritual leader, "the Sultan of Lovers," who referred to himself as "God's light in human form," proudly proclaimed: "My religion and my nation are God." In a famous poem, he explained:

Lo, for I to myself am unknown, now in God's name what must I do?
I adore not the Cross nor the Crescent, I am not a Giaour or a Jew.
East nor West, land nor sea is my home, I have kin nor with angel nor gnome,
I am wrought not of fire nor of foam, I am shaped not of dust nor of dew.

The Mevlana Museum in Konya

I was born not of China afar, not of Saqsin and not in Bulghar;
Not in India, where five rivers are, nor Iraq nor Khurasan I grew.
(Tr. R. A. Nicholson)

He felt little respect for organized religion and stressed the primacy of internal faith and inner allegiance:

I roamed the lands of Christendom from end to end
Searching all over, but He was not on the Cross.

I went into the temples where the Indians worship idols
And the Magians chant prayers to fire - - I found no trace of Him.

Riding at full speed, I looked all over the Kaaba
But He was not at that sanctuary for young and old.

Then I gazed right into my own heart:
There, I saw Him... He was there and nowhere else.

Mevlana was a man of passionate mind, as he expressed it in two eloquent lines:

What miraculous worlds roll within the vast,
The all-embracing ocean of the Mind!
(Tr. R. A. Nicholson)

He combined in himself "the three souls" — sensual, rational, and transcendental (which have also been referred to as animal, cerebral, and inspirational). His mystical life was based on total individualism, the integral or comprehensive personality, the "self" inclusive of God:

Wisdom is light for each step;
Feeling is a sun throughout the road;
Conscience is a voice wide as the horizons.

Mevlana's subjectivity, which embodies the pride of "I am not the bone, but the marrow", finds its cogent echoes in Ludwig Feuerbach's statement: "God is the highest subjectivity of man abstracted from himself. The essential predicates of divinity, such as personality and love, are simply the human qualities men evaluate most highly." Yet Mevlana believes that love unifies all beings: "There are hundreds of thousands of bodies, but only one soul."

Love, according to him, is the ultimate transcendence of human consciousness — analytical and rational, intuitive and holistic, but above all devotional and passionate. In a remarkable poem, he bursts out with the power of love:

If you were patience, I would tear off the veil,
If you were sleep, I would awake the dead,
If you were a mountain, I would consume it with flames,
If you were an ocean, I would drink you down.

In mystic morality, both sin and virtue are transcended. In fact, they are rendered practically meaningless by love's supreme power:

I saw all those people who were the slaves of the world,
I felt true love - - and the whole world became my slave.

Such a sense of triumph, arising from the mystical struggle for perfection, celebrated the human being as an image of God:

Marvellous is the human being,
Strangely wrought in every part,
Made of dust by the creator,
Masterpiece of perfect art.
(Tr. A. J. Arberry)

For Mevlana, life and the universe were in a state of constant flux, a continuing metamorphosis, a dynamic renewal. He promised the faithful he would recreate them:

Come, come, you will never find a friend like me.
Where's a Beloved like me in all the world?
Come, don't waste your life running back and forth.
You are like a dry valley, I am the rain.
You are a city laid waste, I am the architect.
Come!

In one of his *rubai*s, Mevlana described the contrast between the presence and the absence of the loved one:

When I have you, the passions of love make me stay awake;
When you are not with me, I cannot sleep - - I moan, I ache;
I'm awake the night you stay with me and the night you don't - -
But how those two nights are worlds apart, look, for heaven's sake.

The absence of loved ones, the separation from God who is the ultimate and the perfect Beloved, gave the mystics their tragic existence. The *ney*, the traditional reed flute, with its sad, soul-piercing strains, expresses the mystic's yearning to return to beloved God. The opening couplets of the *Mesnevi* capture the reed's moaning:

Listen to the reed, how it tells its tales;
Bemoaning its bitter exile, it wails:

"Ever since I was torn from the reed-beds,
My cries tear men's and women's hearts to shreds.

"Let this separation slit my sad breast
So I can reveal my longing and quest.

"Everyone is my friend for his own part,
Yet none can know the secrets of my heart.

"The flames of love make the reed's voice divine;
It is love's passion that rages in the wine.

"The reed cries with the lovers who fell apart,
It rends the chest and tears open the heart.

"Nothing kills or cures the soul like the reed;
Nothing can crave or console like the reed."

The search for ecstasy, for love, for God is the soul's noble thrust and eventual triumph. Mevlana described the soaring spirit of the dervish as the falcon flying towards God: Its most eloquent expressions are poetry, music, and the *sema* which embodies the unquenchable quest for beauty and perfection. It has no arrival, but the noblest aspiration:

Songs are only a branch of the soul that yearns for Union
The branch and the root are never one and the same.

Music and dance in mystic rites were among Mevlana's impressive innovations. He asked the faithful who came to his academy of mysticism ("The Green Dome") to immerse themselves in music:

Listen with your heart's ear
To all those myriad sounds:
The lovers' cries of passion rise
And resound through the Green Dome.

He clarified that the Whirling Dervishes need no wine nor even music to induce ecstasy:

We need no wine to feel ecstasy or exuberance;
At revelries we need no musicians to make us dance.

Like drunks we lie on the floor, wild with joy, in high heaven;
No boys or belles with cups, no wine, no music for our trance.

When asked why he used music and dance even on such solemn occasions as a funeral, he replied: "When the human spirit, after years of imprisonment in the cage and dungeon of the body, is at last set free, and wings its flight to the source from where it came, isn't this occasion for rejoicing and thanks and dancing?" He expressed this rejoicing in many poems:

While the spirit's sun
Shines gleaming bright,
Like a mote, the mystic
Dances with delight.
(Tr. A. J. Arberry)

His son Sultan Veled wrote of Mevlana's passionate fondness for the *sema*:

Music and dance were his abiding interest;
Day or night, he would celebrate and never rest.
He turned from traditional faith to poesy;
An ascetic at first, he found love's ecstasy.

Mevlana's poetry revels in psychological and philosophical affirmation. He does not seek or crave inner peace. He stresses the primacy of vibrant passion and transcendent ecstasy. Repose or tranquility are not objectives for him, but rather a subdued, subtle color in the spiritual spectrum. His is the supreme combination of Dionysian rapture and Apollonian dignity.

My dusty body
Is heaven's light;
Angels are jealous
To watch my flight.

Cherubim envy
My purity;
Before my valor
All demons flee.
(Tr. A. J. Arberry)

When he invited the mystics to his congregation place in Konya ("This place is the Kaaba for lovers / Whoever comes half leaves full"), he offered them divine music:

They say the reed and the lute that charm our ears
Derive their melody from rolling spheres;
But faith that transcends imagination's bounds
Can see what sweetens all the jangled sounds.

We, who are parts of Adam, heard with him
The song of angels and seraphim.
Our memory, though dull and sad, retains
Some echo still of those unearthly strains.

O, music is the food of souls who love,
Music uplifts our spirit to realms above.
The ashes glow, the latent fires increase:
We listen and are fed with joy and peace.
(Tr. R. A. Nicholson)

Mevlana's invitation to the whirling ritual is exquisite, dramatic, and compelling — and always full of the promise of elevation and enlightenment as evinced by the following synthesis made from several of his poems:

Come!
But don't join us without your music.
We have a celebration here.
Rise and beat the drums.

We are Mansur who said "I am God!"

We are in ecstasy - -
Drunk, but not from wine made of grapes.

Whatever your thoughts are about us,
We are far, far from them.

This is the night of the sema
When we whirl to ecstasy.
There is light now,
There is light, there is light

This is true love,
Which means farewell to the mind.
There is farewell today, farewell.

Tonight each flaming heart is a friend of music.
Longing for your lips,
My heart pours out of my mouth.

Hush!
You are made of feeling and thought and passion;
The rest is nothing but flesh and bone.
We are the soul of the world,
Not heavy or sagging like the body.
We are the spirit's treasure,
Not bound to this earth, to time or space.

How can they talk to us of prayer-rugs and piety?
We are the hunter and the hunted,
Autumn and spring,
Night and day,
Visible and hidden.

Love is our mother.
We were born of Love.

The *sema*, often called *âyin-i şerif* (the blessed ceremony), is an aesthetic sight and experience as well as the mind's passionate thrust. The musicians and singers create an aura of spirituality, of divine poetry. (In the past, before the ceromony, the *canlar*, the "souls," meaning the true mystics, often discussed philosophical concepts, mystical and artistic values, telling Mevlevi stories and interlarding their talks with gracious humor.)

When the dervishes start to whirl rhythmically, their figures, robed in the spare and impeccable tunics with flying skirts, are dynamic and dignified, like living statues. Their blessed ceremony is an act and drama of faith. It is Islamic in many of its themes, yet departs from the mores of establishment Islam or of orthodox Islam particularly in its insistence on the antinomian, direct communion with God and in the way it stresses the whirling ritual. In preparation for the ritual, the dervishes perform, before doing anything else, the ablutions and traditional prayers of Islam. Koranic invocations precede the Sufi chants during the ceremonies.

The whirling, which most dervishes do not consider a form of dance, has some of the attributes of a Dionysian ritual with its roots in Anatolian culture. Its antecedents can also be found in the ancient Turkic shamanistic dances of Central Asia.

Each motion, each gesture has a divine significance. The sudden turns are an attempt to see God in all directions. Thumping the ground symbolizes trampling crass selfhood, crushing egotism. Jumping signifies the desire to soar towards the supreme world. Genuflection is the ultimate expression of abandoning one's soul to God. Opening the arms to the sides is the aspiration to spiritual excellence, the soul's balance, union with God, and eternal bliss. The right arm points heavenward, to God; the left arm down to the earth. This way, the whirling dervish expresses his faith in the world as well as his dream of the beloved Providence. The symbolism has been articulated as follows: "We receive from God, we give out to the people. We never keep any possessions. We soar to the sky, we pour on the ground. Our souls are on the way to God's mercy."

Many of Mevlana's poems capture not only the essence of the mystical spirit itself, but the sensations aroused by the synesthesia of the whirling ritual:

I thump my feet on the floor.
I dance, my soul; I whirl, my world.
Clap your hands, my soul; clap your hands, my world,
Please do - - for the sake of this man in ecstasy.

You may be in a trance,
But don't wreak havoc as in doomsday.
Leave all evil behind.
Place your hand on your heart; but where is the heart?

I abandoned the heart and the soul
And I was left without them in the end.
Where are they, after all?
If there were countless hearts, I would abandon them all.

By means of a whole variety of rhythmic devices and onomatopoeic effects, Mevlana's verse conveys the exquisite excitement of the whirling ceremony:

Come, come. You are the life
Of the inmost soul of the whirling dance.
Come. You are the walking cypress
Of the garden of the whirling dance.

Come. No one like you has ever come
Nor will ever come.

Come. The eyes of the whirling dance have never seen
Nor will ever see anyone like you.

Come. Even the source of the sun
Lies in your shadow.
Yours are the galaxies
In the sky of the whirling dance.

The whirling ritual sings your praises
With a hundred eloquent tongues;
May I offer a few subtle phrases
In the language of the whirling dance?

In the trance of the whirling dance
You soar beyond both worlds:
For its universe
Lies beyond both worlds.

True, heaven's seventh sphere
Has a high roof over it
But the stairway of the whirling dance
Goes way above it.

Whatever is outside of the Beloved
Trample it, crush it.
Yours is the whirling dance
And all that you are is the whirling dance.

What am I to do
If love throws its arms around me?
I too put my arms around it
And take it to my heart when I whirl.

When motes are filled with sunbeams
They all whirl
Without a cry or a moan...
That is the whirling dance.

Come.
Sun of Tabriz is love incarnate.
The whirling dance goes on and on
Dazed with the marvels of love.

Although essentially a dithyrambic ritual, the *sema* has no indignity, no obscenity. No dervish touches another. Sensuality is a private privilege. The "dance" itself is communal, not solitary. In seeking ecstasy, each Sufi is an integral man, purifying his soul, summoning all his passions, having communion with God, without any intermediaries — each man is a world unto himself. As Mevlana states it: "Listening to beautiful sounds, one finds peace of heart and achieves union with God." In all the outward serenity and inner exuberance during the *sema,* the mystic strives to arrive at a state of ecstasy which gives him a glimpse of God:

What nurtures our soul is the whirling dance
Where the loved one emerges in our trance.

Mevlana referred to this spiritual elevation and passionate excitement as a creative surge, as divine inspiration: "The madman of love is above all reason." Antedating Emily Dickinson's "Much madness is divinest sense" by more than six centuries, he wrote:

The secret of madness is the supreme strength of the mind:
Go mad with love if sanity is what you want to find...
Whoever has an inmost heart that stirs with love will leave
The countless estrangements on his arduous path behind.

In one of his most remarkable poems, Mevlana interfused many of the different dimensions, the metamorphoses and even the seeming paradoxes of the ritual and the central mystical experience itself:

You are the sudden doom
You are eternal mercy
And the fire
Whose flames engulf the mind's forest.

Today you came smiling.
You came as the key to the dungeon.
You were bearing God's gift of grace
To those yearning for it.

You drop or raise the curtain on God.
You are our hope, our trusted hero.
You are craved - - and you crave.
You are the beginning and the end.

You bestow life as no one else can.
You are cherished wisdom, delight of knowledge.
All else is false, a mockery.
Others are a disease, you are the remedy.

Revel in ecstasy: Abandon the mind.
Look at this food and push it aside.
All this toil is not worth a meal
Or even a piece of bread.

My mighty hero, whisper in my heart's ear;
Redeem me from heart and soul, my God.
Set me free from this crowd
Of worthless creatures.

Hush! I am in a hurry.
I am under the banners now.
Put away the paper, break the pen.
The cupbearer is here. Come one, come all.

According to the great mystic, one must force and break down the mind's

frontiers in order to witness love's ultimate power and to experience the majesty of God the Beloved:

Joy within joy, the loved one
Tore down the gates of the mind.
You are caught in this blissful ecstasy - -
Revel in the might of God.

In the effusive romantic spirit of Mevlevi mysticism, there are exquisite alternations of overpowering emotional thrusts and soothing tranquility. Significantly, Mevlana expressed not only the thrusts of passion but also the inner peace that emanate from the whirling:

Sema is where the souls of lovers come to rest,
To him who has another heart in his heart it is known best.

The man of the spirit is also the man of reality. Enamored as he was of flights of mystic fantasy, Mevlana remained involved in the welfare of the people of his city, in social justice, in affairs of the state. That is why he was

"Mevlana" (guide, lord, master) not only for his disciples but also for laymen. He denigrated temporal power:

Be the slave of someone whose heart glitters
Instead of wearing the crown of the Sultans.

In a memorable couplet, he posited the worthlessness of public office:

Lordship is hardly worth the pain of being deposed;
You might enjoy it for a day, but you'll shudder for a century.

He maintained that his spiritual power is superior to royalty:

I am not one of those kings who must step down
From the throne to take the ride in a coffin.

Mevlana, according to legend, sometimes defied and took to task an unjust sultan or vizier. Once, when the Sultan sought his guidance, he answered scathingly: "What could I possibly tell you? They expected you to be the shepherd. Yet you are the wolf. They wanted you to be the guard. You turned out to be the thief."

The opening lines of his *Fih i Mafih*, a work in prose, proclaim the scholar's independence from political power. Elaborating on a *hadith* (tradition) of the Prophet, Mevlana asserts: "The deplorable scholar is the one who receives assistance, support and strength from the lords. He is the worst who does his scholarship with the anticipation of handouts, of respect, of position and with the fear of the lords." Because he would never compromise his intellectual sovereignty, Mevlana reportedly lived and died a man without acquisitions or assets. He expressed his pride over this, according to the *Manakıb al-Arifin* (Legends of the Saints) by the 14th-Century biographer Aflaki, to none other than the mighty Grand Vizier Parvana. At an official dinner which Mevlana attended, a bowl of rice with a purse containing gold coins was placed before him on Parvana's orders. The Sufi leader contemptuously rejected the grant and recited the following couplet to the Grand Vizier and his retinue:

Thank God, I have no desire for delicacies or sweets;
I find no value in a purse of gold or a golden bowl.

He spurned material pleasures and gains. For the mystic who triumphed by divesting himself of worldly possesions, poverty was a matter of pride:

Poverty is heart's ease
All else is the soul's disease.

Poverty is the sole
Treasure, and spirit's goal.
(Tr. A. J. Arberry)

For Mevlana, the "good man is he who serves the people." He detested the praise and the panegyrics offered to unjust rulers: "If you so much as try to extol an evil man, God's lofty spheres convulse." In a remarkable lyric ode, he vented his fury on kings who oppress the poor people:

I am such a dark night that I am angry at the moon;
I am such a stark-naked pauper that I am angry at the Sultan.

They try to deceive me with gold or high station or troops;
I want no gold, no matter what, I am angry at power and position.

He advised the rulers to avoid being "a burden on the people," "to march free like a horse instead of being a carcass that the people must carry on their backs."

Mevlana's writings are full of criticism leveled at arrogant lords, rulers who take bribes, officials who scorn the people, merchants who cheat their customers; they contain painful depictions of cities destroyed and villages ruined, severed heads, children stoning madmen, hunger and famine. He often advocated the principles of social justice, made references to communality of property, and stood against dogmatic formalism. For him, a theft committed by a man oppressed by poverty was a lesser crime than the one committed by oppressors who keep the people in abject poverty. Once a burglar stole a valuable rug from Mevlana's academy. The burglar was later caught and brought before Mevlana, who said: "He must have stolen because of need," and bought the rug from the burglar.

In Mevlevi ethics, intellectual achievement and enlightenment play a focal role. Love and intellect, for Mevlana, are complements of each other, and their absence is often closely linked to injustice and evil.

Mevlana spoke out against conformism, loveless doctrine, the preachers and defenders of the narrowest strictures, and fanatics hell-bent to reduce religion to austere, joyless, stultifying vacuities. When criticized for his use of song in the Mevlevi ceremony, he retorted: "The song in the *sema* is like faith in prayers." Seyyid Şerefeddin, a dogmatist, once took Mevlana to task for having said: "From the viola d'amore we hear the tunes of the gate of Paradise," and added that he also hears tunes but they have no such effect on him. Mevlana reportedly gave the following satirical reply: "Of course. We hear from the viola d'amore the tunes of the opening of the gate of Paradise. He hears the sounds of the closing." The mystic leader also stressed the vital importance of feeling in science and scholarship: "Only if they enlighten the heart and transform man into a person of feelings can science and scholarship yield benefits. If they affect only our physical being without exalting the spirit, they are just a burden."

Mevlana gave women an exalted place: "Woman is not a creature, but creator." In the Mevlevi movement women often found acceptance and fulfillment. Particularly at the time of Ulu Arif Çelebi, who was Sultan Veled's son and Mevlana's grandson, they took part in the ceremonies and the *sema*.

It is said that Mevlana, who was not known to have had much interest in poetry earlier, took up verse as his major intellectual vehicle after meeting Şems. Another speculation asserts that he did so to please his circle of colleagues and disciples. According to a third theory, he found poetry essential to disseminate his ideas to the larger community, which had a penchant for verse. Regardless of the basic motivation, the fact remains that Mevlana started composing poetry at the age of 37 and, in the period of about thirty years until his death, he produced a corpus of verse which is nothing short of the miraculous in both quantity and quality. In his prose work *Fih i Mafih* he referred to poetry as a means rather than an end, since his purpose was to instruct and inspire. Inasmuch as it was often ecstasy that prevailed in his poems, the prosody and the rhymes seemed to be of secondary importance. Sometimes he openly complained about the stringencies of classical meters and the strait jacket of stanzaic forms. Formal devices, in his view, were restrictive — even the words themselves fell short of transcendent significance:

Eternal King from whose couplets and odes I am set free,
Pentameters and tetrameters had nearly murdered me.
The flood took away all those deceiving rhymes in one thrust,
Leaving them to lesser poets whose heads have a thick crust.

He praised the supremacy of feeling, passion and love over form:

I sit around racking my brains to find this or that rhyme.
My loved one tells me: "You should think of my face all the time."
We are together now, relax; these rhymes have no value.
I find the rhyme and reason of the happy state in you.

In one poem, he traced his progress from consuming love to the renunciation of dogma and rational life to the poetic arts:

When the flames of love for which I had yearned
Struck my breast and all love in my heart burned,

The mind, the school, the books became things I spurned - -
And then, to verses and rhymes I turned.

Regardless of such protestations, poetry served for him as the embodiment of philosophical experience, the supreme fiction, the transcendent reality. Like mystic love, it was conceived of by Mevlana as its own perfection — the perfection of the ideal. His best verses conform to the famous dictum of Archibald MacLeish: "a poem should not mean / but be." Mevlana's poetry has not only profound meanings but also a concrete structural existence — not mere form — with an architectonic splendor.

Heightened by effusive lyricism, combining high classical style with the vernacular, his language is rich in abstractions as well as objectified and concretized statements, interlarded with folk sayings and proverbs. The fervor with which he unfurls his mystic passions safeguards his poems from the dry didacticism which characterizes so much other mystical writings:

This is the day: Whirl around your love. Nothing is amiss:
Whirl. After all, no one can blame the frenzied heart for this.
No mere battle, but life-and-death combat, ordeal of fire - -
This is the night of reunion, embrace, and nuptial bliss.

His poetic art, in many respects, is truly Platonic, but goes far beyond the Platonic norms and concepts: with its *furor poeticus*, it is the "poetry of inspiration" par excellence. It is "poetry as hermetic symbolism" at its best, with a marvelous coherence of myths, images, metaphors, and the interaction of the occult, the obscure, the concrete, and the worldly. It is "poetry as instruction" of supreme values — good, beautiful, true — which are all aspects and attributes of love and of God. It is also *mimesis*, the highest form of imitation, whereby the poet seeks to simulate, and to emulate, the divine archetype. Mevlana's poetry embraces all of these categories and creates a norm which evokes Shelley's words: "Poetry is the center and circumference of all knowledge."

Ultimately poetry and love become identical and mutually inclusive in Mevlana's mysticism. In his verse we find his encompassing visions of life and death, and his ethical concepts.

Peace, in his view, was a focal virtue to be nurtured and defended for the individual and the community. In his lifetime he witnessed the ravages of the Mongol invasion and the Crusades. World peace was a supreme ideal for him. He stood against injustice and tyranny: "When weapons and ignorance come together, pharoahs arise to devastate the world with their cruelty," an observation that still holds true more than 700 years after Mevlana's death. One of his most eloquent couplets proclaims:

Whatever you think of war, I am far, far from it;
Whatever you think of love, I am that, only that, all that.

It is love and the true lover that live the everlasting life. That is why he invited lovers to join the magnificent exodus:

O lovers, lovers!
This is the time of exodus from the world.
In my heart's ear rumble
The huge drums of the great migration.

Proclaiming with the pride of the true mystic that "I was created by God from His elixir of love / Even if I die and my body decays, I shall still be that love," he defied death:

What if death wields its sword, cuts off my head, and leaves me slain - -
I shall still shoot up from the ground like countless spikes of grain.
Just as the ears of corn can find new life in the good earth,
Some day, the human grain, too, shall sprout from the dust again.

Mystics welcome, and passionately strive for, "dying before death" to attain the ultimate reality and beauty of love:

We are the enemies of our own selves
We are the friends of our killers;
We have plunged deep into the sea
Whose waves are buffeting us to death.

The fearsome Angel of Death
Would not dare kill the lovers,
Only love, profound love
Can kill the lovers who fall into his hands.

Life is a breeze the loved one takes away
Wine is the life the loved one grants,
Rescues the soul's falcon and sets it free,
And slays the raven of despair.

Death confronts man hundreds of times each day
But the true lovers of God
Surrender themselves to Death without cause
Even though Death does not confront them.

Mevlana gave a new significance to *vitae mori ac vivere morti*. The mystic, according to him, "dies and returns to life every instant." That is why he asserts: "You have a deathless soul. Why on earth are you afraid of death? / You possess the light of God. How can you fit into a grave?" The real death, the abject death is "when the heart falls asleep." For the heart that remains awake in love, death is nothing more than blissful silence, the eloquent quiet. The Mevlevis refer to the "dead" dervishes merely as *hâmuşan* (the quiet ones).

Mevlana often invited the believer to true death which is the life of love, of eternity:

Die, die. Living this love, die.
When you die of this love, you shall find life.

Die, die. Have no fear of death:
Rise all the way to heaven and hold the skies.

Die, die. Break away from the selfish soul,
The chain that holds you bound like a captive.

Take hold of a mace to tear down the dungeon.
Demolish it and you will all become sultans and lords.

Die, die, in the presence of the loveliest Sultan.
If you do, you will all become sultans of great fame.

Die, die. Come out from behind that cloud;
Once you do, you will all become full moons.

Hush! Keep quiet. Silence is the speech of death.
You flee from silence beacuse you cling on to life.

The liberation of the spirit that comes from death in love is, according to Mevlana, both eternal justice and the highest form of happiness:

With death the man of faith attains real life and true justice:
On the immaculate soul death bestows its calm and bliss...
The embrace of reunited lovers inflicts no pain;
Only the man who never knew death in life perishes.

The sense of immortality derived from love interlocks Mevlana's romantic spirit and system of ethics:

In this Ocean, there is no death,
No despair, no sadness or anxiety.
This Ocean is love, boundless love:
This is the Ocean of kindness and generosity.

Mevlana's words on the eve of his death are an affirmation of continuing life: "Light is about to reunite with Light. I stripped myself of selfhood, and He stripped Himself of His image. I am now teetering at the edge of the Land of Reunion." His poems often evoke the immortality achieved by love:

If I should die
I bid you carry me
To where my love might lie
There let me be.

And if she would give
My cold lips just one kiss,
Believe me, I would live
Again by this.
(Tr. A. J. Arberry)

The night of Mevlana's death, whose anniversary is observed on December 17th each year at Konya, is called *Şeb-i Arus* (the wedding night):

Death is reunion with God:
The night of my death
Will be a bridal night,
The nuptial with supreme love.

In Mevlana's vision, death was the ultimate triumph:

When my coffin starts its journey to the grave
Don't think I am unhappy to leave this world.
When you lower me into the pit, don't weep
Because that is a curtain behind which lies
Peaceful Paradise.

Mevlana's funeral occasioned the saddest *sema*, because Konya had lost its great spiritual guide and Anatolia one of its dazzling cultural figures. It was at the same time the most joyous, because the greatest mystic of them all had at last reached his beloved God. Not only were Moslems crying at the funeral, but Christians (including Greeks and Armenians) and Jews, as well — men of different creeds, languages, ethnic origins. They had come to revere him as

their own, beacuse he had revered them and their prophets as his own. He symbolized, as he continues to do, the unity of mankind. "There are," he said, "hundreds of thousands of bodies — but only One Soul." Mevlana himself did not initiate the Mevlevi Order. It was done in his name after his death by his son Sultan Veled and some of his disciples. Bemoaning rifts and enmities, Mevlana called for peace, for a united world transcending schisms, for love of man and love of God.

Mevlana had a humanist, universalist, humanitarian vision: "I am," he declared, "a temple for all mankind."

Like a compass I stand firm with one leg on my faith
And roam with the other leg all over the seventy-two nations.

Seventy-two nations hear of their secrets from us:
We are the reed whose song unites all nations and faiths.

Regrettably, no scholar has made a study of Mevlana's humanism. His Mausoleum, which has come to be known as "the stronghold of the lovers," even today inspires thousands of visitors — Moslem, Christian, Jewish and others. They find in "The Green Dome" a vast heritage of spiritual splendor, an overwhelming aesthetic delight, and an engrossing humanistic ethic. One of his famous *rubai*s invites all human beings, regardless of creed, ethnic background, social status, or nationality, to his shrine:

Come, come again, whoever, whatever you may be, come:
Heathen, fire-worshiper, sinner of idolatry, come.
Come even if you broke your penitence a hundred times,
Ours is not the portal of despair or misery, come.

Proclaiming that "my faith and my nation are God," Mevlana made a plea for universal brotherhood in a world torn asunder by conflicting ideologies, sectarian divisions, religious strife, and jingoistic nationalism. One of his universalist statements is remarkable for its age: "Hindus, Kipchaks, Anatolians, Ethiopians — they all lie peacefully in their graves, separately, yet the same color." "The Sultan of Lovers" also wrote one of the most eloquent lines of ecumenism:

In all mosques, temples, churches I find one shrine alone.

Mevlana has been claimed by several countries and cultures — Iran, Turkey, Afghanistan, the Arabs, and the Moslem communities of the Soviet Union — on grounds of genealogy, birthplace, language, cultural orientation, adopted country, burial place, and the territory of impact. The strongest are those advanced by Iran and Turkey, with considerable justification. Yet a close scrutiny of biographical and other historical documents support few of these claims in any convincing way. The internal references found in his work show that he wanted no "national" identification or "citizenship" in terms of our modern concepts and definitions. He sought, rather, to belong to mankind and to transcend religious schisms and national allegiances. His mystic spirit can and must be claimed not by one country, one culture, one religion, but by all humanity.

The mystic love, aesthetics of ethics, humanism and humanitarianism of Mevlana Celaleddin Rumi strike a vital chord in the world today. His is a mind of passion for all seasons, a climate of all the sacred affirmations in the human heart. When all is said and done, it is conceivable, beyond the tragic eras and the happy ages of history, that the most profound truth, perhaps the only irreducible value inherent in human existence is the one expressed so eloquently in a line from a poem by Mevlana: "Live in love's ecstasy, for love is all that exists."

MEVLANA MINIATURES

"The most detailed and authentic account" of Mevlana Celaleddin Rumi's life, as noted by the renowned Orientalist Edward G. Browne, may be found in *Manaqib al Arifin* by Shams al-Din Ahmad al-Aflaki,* written in Persian. "It is true," Browne observes, "that many of the miraculous achievements of Jalalu'd-Din and his predecessors and successors which are recorded in this work are quite incredible... but it was begun only forty-five years after the Master's death (viz., in A.D. 1318) and finished in 1353; and was, moreover, compiled by a disciple living on the spot from the most authoritative information available."

Aflaki's work featuring the life and legends of the Moslem gnostics and mystics was condensed and recast in Persian verse in 1540 by Abd al-Wahhab ibn Jalal al-Din Muhammad al-Hamadani, who gave his version the title of *Sawaqib al-Manaqib* (The Luminaries of the Legends). Two chapters of this work dealing with Mevlana and his father were translated into Turkish by Mahmud Dede, a Konya Mevlevi sheikh and a reciter of Mevlana's *Mesnevi.* Mahmud Dede went to Istanbul in 1588 or 1589 and presented his translation to Sultan Murad III, who was known as a patron of literature and miniature painting. Impressed with the two chapters, the Sultan commissioned him to do a complete Turkish version. Returning to Konya, Mahmud Dede finished his work in 1590, giving it the title of *Tercüme-i Menakıb-ı Sevakıb* (variously transliterated as Tarcuma-i Manaqib al-Sawakib or Thawaqib), meaning "Translation of the Legends of the Luminaries"). Several dozen manuscripts of this work, produced in a variety of calligraphic styles between the end of the 16th Century and the beginning of the 20th, are in libraries in Turkey and abroad. The copy in The Morgan Library collection in New York (No. 466) contains 29 miniatures. Topkapı Palace Museum in Istanbul has a copy (Revan No. 1479) containing 22 miniatures. The reproductions appearing on the following pages feature 22 miniatures from the Topkapı Palace book and 2 from the Morgan Library album.

* Sir James Redhouse (d.1892) published an abridged English translation (entitled "Acts of the Adepts") in his 1881 volume *The Mesnevi, Book the First.*
Clemens Huart's French translation, *Les saints des derviches tourneurs,* was published in Paris, 1918-1922.

The colophon of the Morgan Library copy is missing, and the Topkapı copy provides no data about the artist(s) or the studio — or even about the place where these paintings were produced. Prof. Nurhan Atasoy and Dr. Filiz Çağman, in their impressive study entitled *Turkish Miniature Painting,* speculate that the work was probably done in Konya at the Mevlevi congregation-place where Mahmud Dede served as a sheikh and did his translation. They observe that "the provincial style comes over strongly throughout the manuscript" and its "free intimate atmosphere" contrasts with the "official style of the palace school" in İstanbul.

The reproduction sizes are identical to the original measurements. Unlike most of the miniatures by the Ottoman palace artists, these tend to break out of their frames, liberating their forms and perspectives in a thrust of the mystical spirit which transcends stringent limitations.

The miniatures, ranging from poise and tranquillity to vibrant action, constitute a major collection in the corpus of Mevlana paintings. They unfurl a fascinating panorama of the great Sufi master's life, deeds, and "miracles".

Talat Sait Halman

بسم الله الرحمن الرحيم

بر حمدك عظيم نورى كه يوزبيك درديجى كونلك كنشى كبى كنش
آنك جمال باكمالنك آيدنلغندن بر ذرّه اولماز وبرشاما هتابك
ماهتابى كه بو فلك بدرى آنك هلالنك خيالنه ايرشمكه يول
بولماز ودخى مناقب ثواقبنك معاينيسى لآلى بينك كه كوكلر
طبقه‌لرنده اولان نجوم آنلرك نور ويرمسى زماننده صدف
خزفلر كبى بلكه هر بريسى مقام ومرتبه سنده خزف پاره‌لر كبى كورينور
وحضرت مولانا جلال الدين مظهر قدرت مولى ومظهر عزت خير البشر

بو یونلر بنده صارلمش ایدی نطقه کلوب دیدیلر که أشهد
ان لا اله الا الله واشهد ان محمد عبده ورسوله
ایلدیکك تحقیقه بزشاهدز اشته حشر اولوب شهادت

بومرتبه قوللق عرض ایدرلردی مقام عبودیتده اولنلرك حق وصفاسی
تعبیر اولنمز بویله نقل اولنور که بر کوزسن دایما حضرت مولانا عشقنه
دیو سائللر عادتی اوزره هر کسیدن بر نسنه استردی اتفاق حضرت مولانایه
راست کلدی جرّ ایلدی حضرتك بلنده بر کمری وار ایدی اول سائله ویردی
اخی چوبان نامنه اعیاندن اول اعمایه یوز آلتون ویرین اول کمری بکا
ویرسون دیدی قبول اتمیوب بیك آلتون اولورسه ده ویرمزم وصیتم
اولدر که سترهٔ آخرت ایدیم دیوب اول کیجه اغلیوب یا ربّ العزّه بنم جانمی آل

حضرت مولانا سنده مقابله قلدی طایوتجلی اول واصل خدمتنه
دخی انجلین ایلدی والحاصل مابین ده اوتوز نوبت راهب

حاضر اولدیلر اما هر کلن کمسنه اوکنه بر اعلا موم یقدی آخر
حضرت مولانا کلدی و یارانه بیوردیکه بزم اوکومزه بر کوچک موم
قویوك خلق جمع اولیجق حضرت سلطانك اوکنده اولان مومك

یا پشوب دید مکه قونیه شهردن بر محتاج الله عشقنه بکا دستگیر
اول قافله دن قالدم بیور دیکه چون همشهریمزا ایمش سن غمیه دیوب

کوزکی یومردیدی امرنی قبول ایدوب کوزیمی یومدم ینه آچدم کوردم
که قافله ده کندی رفیقلرم اراسنده یم اشته بو خذمتلر که کورسز اول

خیمه سنی بر ایوك دیبنه قورمشلریدی انك اوستنه چقوب
نمازه شروع ایلدی اول حالده حضرت مولانایی کوروب
باچویه خبر ویردیلر که برمایی قفتانلی دخانی عمامه‌لی کمسنه نمام
فراغت و هیبتله نمان قلار. امّا هیبتدن لشکر بربرنه قارشدی

تجارت ایچون اسکندریه‌یه کتمشدم اتفاقی کمومز کردابه دوشدی
کمی موزکن دابه دوشدی کمی ده اولنلرک هر بریسی پیرلرینه قربان نذر
ایدوب خلاص رجا ایلدیلر بو فقیر ده حضرت مولانایی شفیع کتوردم
یا مولانا سن یتیش دیو آشکاره فریاد ایلدم همان حضرت مولانا حاضر اولدی

مشغول اولدی حضرت مولانایه معلوم اولوب همان بر سهمناك
بانك ایدب بو آیة کریمهٔ قراءت ایلدی ایحب احدکم ان یاکل لحم اخیه

حضرت سلطان چته کلدی جمیعًا احواله مطلع اولوب اهل بیتنك
شفاعتنی قبول ایدوب عفو ایلدی اولجانور دخی تجدید توبه ایدی
بر دانه انجی بولدی که لطافتندن آدم حیران اولوردی بعده یراوپدی

ایدرسن نیجه‌یه دك تاج وخرقه سن معرّف اولور قصد وهمّت
ایدك سن جامه‌لر یکوزه معرّف اوله سن ظاهر لباسکوزسن معرّف
اولدوغی کبی دیوب تنبیه ایلدیکه باطنکزدخی معانی ومعارف

١٢٥
صغیره صادر اولدی فی الحال ینه استغفار ایلدم اول کون حضرت
مولانا سماعده بنم بقمه محکم بیشوب وشهادت برمغی ایله اشارت ایلدیکه
ای ولد صادق اوج کره اکر فراغت ایلمزسك سن بلورسن دیوب
زیاده تنبیه ایلدی امدی ای یاران پرهیز واحتیاط اوزره اولك

وزیر دشوار کلوب زیاده مناقشه ایلدیلر حتی خدمت فوت
اولمق زمانی اولدی وموکل که پادشاه بو خصوصه تعیین ایلمشدی
وزیر دستی المدین یول ویرمدی آخر بر اطاعت لازم کلدی بیجان اکوز
ویر دستی بوغازنه آصوب ویری ارقه سنه کوتروب سلطانك خدمتنه

تاخیر ایدر آنك حسندن بهره مند اولورلر دیوب امدی بنم کیج
کلمکدن مرادم بو درکه سز منتظر اولوب وخدمتکوزده اولان نیازمند
اولان آدملر زیاده ذوق ایدوب فایده اله کتوره لر دیوب انواع

مولاسلطان العلمانك زيارتنه وارمشيدي زيارتي تمام ايمش
كلوركن اوكوز همان مولانايي كورنجه خدمتنه وارب يوزني يره سوردي
جد لحركت ايميوب قالدی حضرت مولانا مبارك الني ارقه سنه ديورنه
سورب اوغشردی والتفات ايلدی بعده قصابلر كلوب بولديلر آلدی

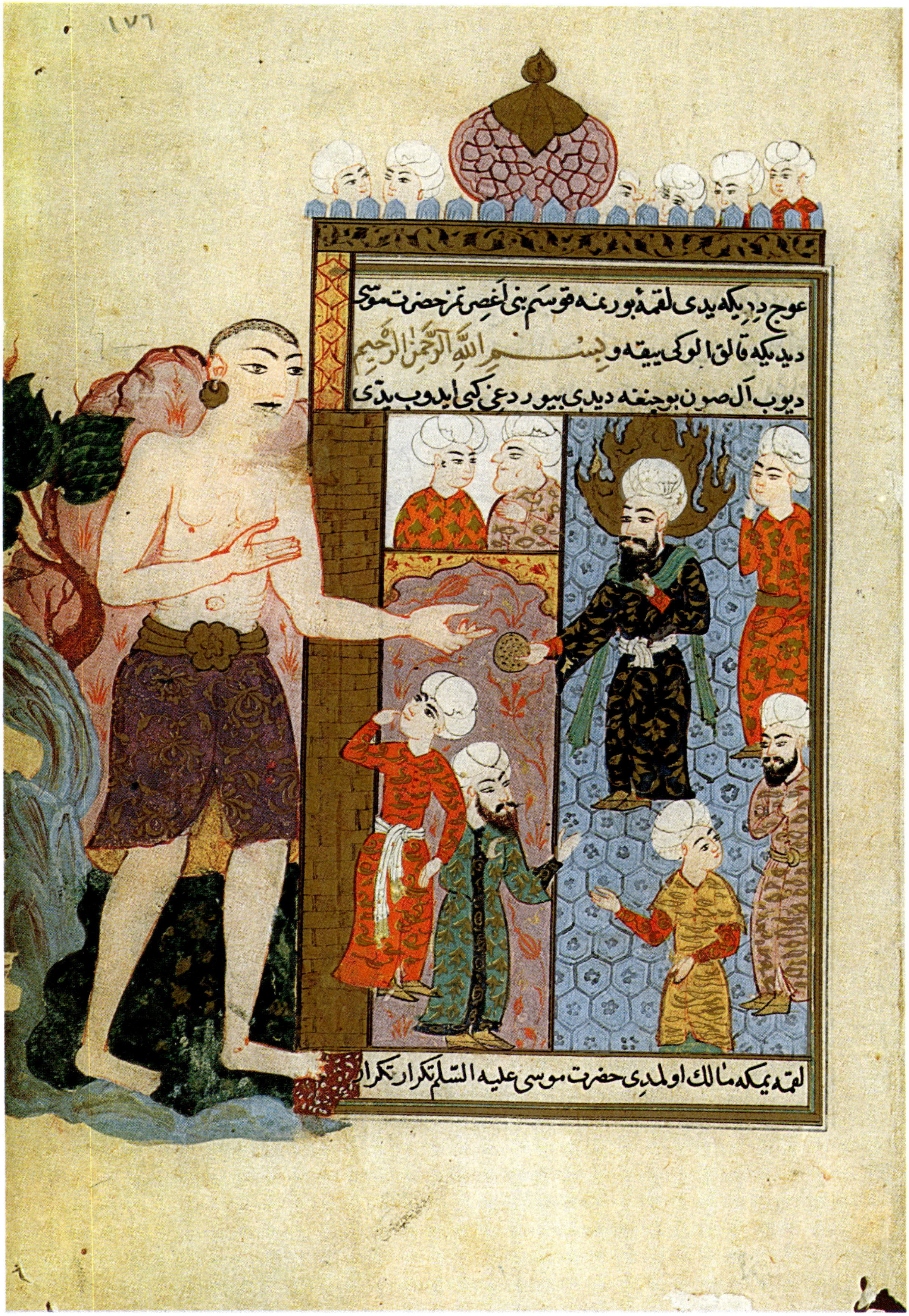

عوج دریکه یدی لقمه بورینه قوسم بنی اغصیتر حضرت موسی
دیدیکه قالق الوکی بیقه و بسم الله الرحمن الرحیم
دیوب آل صون بو جنغه دیدی بیور دعی کبی ایدوب یدی
لقمه یمکه مالك اولمدی حضرت موسی علیه السلم تکرار تکرار

٢١٥
اوردی كه اهل فسادك يديسی ده لا يعقل ولوب يقلديلر
عقله كليجك اول سلطانك برفج قطره ندن غيری نشان بولمديلر

نظر ایدوب کوردیکه جمیعاً آلت دکان آلتون اولمش احوالی تبدیل
اولوب زرکوبلغی ترک ایدوب دکانی یغما ایلدی وحضرت مولانا

هیچ سویلمدی حتی یاران فریاد ایدوب سؤال ایلدیلر نچون رضا
کوسترسز دیدیلر جواب بیود دیکه برزم سرّمز بهاء الدین درکه
الولد سرابیه
یه مطابقدر اما علاء الدین تیز کیدر دیوب کشف

يدی خط طولانی چکدی ویدی دخی عرضنه چکدی وآخر یازدیکه
العاقل یکفیه الاشاره همان اول زمان امیر عارف مبارک

٢٦١
كلدیکه عجبا مرضنه ضرر واقع اوله‌می دیو فکر ایدرکن چلبی کشف
ایدوب بیوردیکه شمدیدنصکره فارغ اول و سماعه مشغول اول
تا صحت بولوب مرضندن خلاص اوله‌سن دیوب تسلی ایلدی اخی
محمد همان مبارك ایاغنه دوشوب فریاد ایلدی و اول مرضندن

سركردان اولان بيچاره لری زلال وصالكدن محروم ايلمه ديوب
كوناكون قسم ذكر ايدرك حق سبحانه وتعالى عنايت ايدب كناره

عمرنی ضایع ایلمزدی بلکه نه ایچون خلق اولندوغن فکر ایدردی
دینجه حکیم سنایی دیوانه نک کلماتن استماع ایدب متغیر الحال

بو غدیر حتی اولر مانده مولانا مولانا دیورک جان تسلیم ایلدی حضرت خداوندگار
اولر مانده مبارک مدرسه سنده سماعده ایدی مبارک برمقلرینی قولاقلرینه محکم دیقدی
بر نیچه زماندنصکره بو غزلی بیوردی
نگفتمت مرو آنجا که آشنات منم
درین سراب فنا چشمهٔ حیات منم

فاضه معینه سی اولادوغل تنک علی التمام والکمال اهمالیز خدمتن ایدر
همچنین قانون سماع وصفا جمعه دنصکره واثنین وخمیس قنده تلاوت
مجید دنصکره قرآت مثنوی معنوی کوینده کان تقسیم غزل سپازندکان
وقوالان باب قدوم نوازلق ایدوب عاشقان وصادقان چرخ ورقص

LIST OF MINIATURES

Sawaqib al-Manaqib (TSM R. 1479)

Sawaqib al-Manaqib (The Morgan Library, New York. No. 466)

SEMA:
THE SPIRITUAL CONCERT OF THE MEVLEVIS

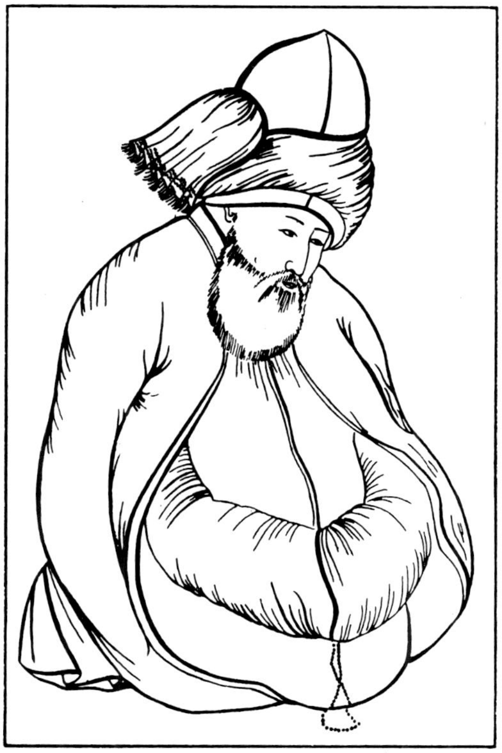

by Metin And

The Mevlevi dervishes performing for the sultan. (TSM H. 1344)

Whirling Dervishes (19th Century)

A very large number of dervish orders and sub-orders were established by the Sufis of the Ottoman Empire.One of the most influential of these monastic sects, known as *tarikat* (Arabic: *tariqa*, meaning "the path"), was the Mevlevi Order which came to be known in the West as "The Whirling Dervishes" in reference to the ritual whirling they perform as part of their ceremonies. The Mevlevi dervishes, who are the followers of the great Anatolian Islamic mystic poet-philosopher Mevlana Celaleddin Rumi, were opposed by the austerity and rigidity of orthodox Islam. Although the Koran articulates no interdiction against music and dancing, Moslem fanatics traditionally waged a relentless war against them. Time-honored secular music and dances, as well as the litanies, chants and the whirling rituals of the various Sufi sects, survived through the centuries in spite of sustained pressure from the zealots.

The Sufi orders, headed by a leader (*şeyh, pir, baba*), offered in their cloisters (*tekke*) pious retreat, meditation and contemplation, prayers and fasting, and other practices of traditional as well as unorthodox Islam, to the acolytes and initiates (*mürid*). Among the numerous esoteric Sufi sects, the Rufai, Nakşibendi, Mevlevi, Melami, Saadi, Kadiri and Bektaşi are well known. Not all of them, however, have dancing as part of their rituals. The Rufai, Kadiri, Halveti, Bayrami, Gülşeni, and Uşşaki practice the *devr*, literally

meaning rotation, which consists of turns that the dancers make in a circle while holding each other. In some other sects, e.g., Nakşibendi, the members remain seated in a circle and make simultaneous movements. The ceremonies of some other orders are contemplative and a few sects, like the Hamzavi and Melami, hold secret rituals which may not be seen by outsiders.

Extensive literature exists in Arabic, Persian, and Turkish on the lawfulness or unlawfulness of music and dancing.[1] Although dance was considered altogether reprehensible by conservative interpreters of Islam, the heterodox Sufis, who stressed direct contact with God, looked upon dance in a more tolerant way and cited occasions when it was regarded as permissible. Some prominent Sufi thinkers, among them the remarkable theologian and jurist al-Ghazzali (d. 1111) in his *Ihya Ulum ad-Din* (Revival of Religious Sciences)[2], formulated an apologia for dancing under certain circumstances. He explains very ably that melodies which stir up joy and emotion, and their manifestation through poetry, song, dance and movement are praiseworthy. He emphasizes that certain laws laid down by the Koran regarding dancing point out that time, place, social usage, one's ability, and other circumstances should be taken into consideration when dancing takes place. He mentions the sanction of singing and dancing, watching the dancing of the

Abyssinians, and the Prophet's permission to listen to music and song on festival days. He describes one instance when the Prophet found dancing permissible, and two others when it was found praiseworthy, but with the comment that, in the opinion of the Prophet, dancing is not proper for a notable person. Al-Ghazzali also discusses the relationship between the dancer's state of mind and the dancing, noting that only genuine ecstasy will make his movements light and brisk.

Similarly, commenting on the odes of Ibn al-Farid (d. 1235), a scholar makes the following remark: "Many Sufis looked with disfavor on the ecstatic dance, which is a well-known feature of the *sema*, cf. the saying *al-raqs naqs* (dancing is a fault). Ibn al-Farid justifies it on the ground that it is an anodine to the fever of the soul; its violent movements calm the agitating reminiscences awakened by music and rock the soul to rest."[3] Early Sufi writers, e.g., Sarraj, Qushayri, and Hujwiri, do not agree with him in thinking that the practice of the *sema* is beneficial. For instance Hujwiri makes the following comment:

> You must know that dancing (*raqs*) has no foundation either in the religious law (of Islam) or in the path (of Sufism), because all reasonable men agree that it is a diversion when it is in earnest, and an impropriety (*laghwi*) when it is in jest. None of the Shaykhs has commended it or exceeded due bounds therein, and all the traditions cited in its favour by anthopomorphists (*ahl-i hashw*) are worthless. But since esctatic movements and the practices of those who endeavour to induce esctasy (*ahl-i tawajud*) resemble it, some frivolous imitators have indulged in it immoderately and have made it a religion. I have met with a number of

common people who adopted Sufism in the belief that it is this (dancing) and nothing more. Others have condemned it altogether. In short, all foot-play (*pay-bazî*) is bad in law and reason, by whomsoever it is practised, and the best of mankind cannot possibly practise it; but when the heart throbs with exhilaration and rapture becomes intense and the agitation of ecstasy is manifested and conventional forms are gone, that agitation (*idthirab*) is neither dancing nor foot-play nor bodily indulgence, but a dissolution of the soul. Those who call it "dancing" are utterly wrong. It is a state that cannot be explained in words: "without experience no knowledge."[4]

The Syrian jurist Ibn Taimiyya (d. 1328) was especially prominent in voicing his opposition. He wrote many pamphlets and *fetvas*[5] condemning eminent Sufis and their practice of seeking ecstasy through music and dancing, along with other practices, as contrary to the law.[6]

The dancing of these orders was condemned by the orthodox Moslems, and particularly by the Ulema, sometimes on the grounds of being improper or even sinful. Occasionally the Ulema tried to suppress the dances on political grounds. All this is well explained by the Turkish scholar Katib Çelebi (1609-1657):

The orthodox Ulema have classed those whirlings as "dancing," and have pronounced it forbidden, branding as infidels those who hold it permissible. The Sufis begin by saying that the definition of "dancing" is not applicable to it. They continue thus: "The cyclic motion is a form of motion — there is no harm in it from the point of view of the public good." They adduce the examples of the Ethiopian dance and the whirling of Ali, and say: "The man who takes one side in a dogmatic dispute is not to be declared an infidel." The real purpose of the Ulema's prohibition is to protect the State, for in the past States have suffered much from the Sufis: witness in particular the rise of the Safavids in Persia. Consequently there has been harshness and severity, with the resultant advantage, from the point of view of the State, that the spiritual ardour which tended to increase the number of disciples and to attract adherents has diminished.[7]

Of all the influences from the East on Turkish dancing, possibly the most pervasive is the Central Asian shamanistic influence, which is felt on the dancing of the religious orders and quasi-religious social dancing of the village Alevi. This is especially true of the Bektaşi and Kalender dervishes. The latter are an irregular and unorthodox order of wandering dervishes who belong to the rural heterodoxy. The distinction between rural and urban becomes more pronounced in this context. Although the Bektaşi Order later became almost urban, it made a very strong impact over the nomadic heterodox tribes and their dancing. Some dervish orders even have a Central Asian origin, such as the Halveti and Nakşibendi. For instance, a well-known orientalist, Arminius Vambéry, who travelled extensively both in Central Asia and Turkey and was interested in Ottoman relations with Central Asia, gives an account of dervish dancing he witnessed in Samarkand:

> What the dervishes are able to do during the ecstasy caused by Zikr, I had once an opportunity of witnessing in Samarkand. In Dehbid, close to the tomb of the Makhdun Aazam, one of these howling companies had grouped themselves around the Pir (chief) of that district. At first they contented themselves with repeating the formula in a natural tone of voice and almost in measured time. The chief was lost in the deepest thought; all eyes and ears were fixed upon him; and every motion of his hand and breath he drew was audible, and encouraged his followers to utter wild and louder ejaculations. At last he seemed to awake from his sleep-like reflections, and as soon as he raised his head all the dervishes jumped up from their seats like possessed beings. The circle was broken and the different members began to dance in undulating motions; but hardly did the chief stand upon his feet than the enthusiastic dancers became so terribly excited that I who had to imitate all their wild antics became almost frightened. They were flying about, constantly dancing, right and left and thither, some leaving the soft meadow getting upon the rough stones, constantly dancing, till the blood began to run freely from their feet. Still they kept on their mad excitement, till most of them fell fainting to the ground.[8]

Vambery also gives a description accompanied by an illustration of the dance by the Nakşibendi dervishes miming the heroic actions of the prophets and of famous warriors at the mosque of Mesdjid-i Divanbeghi.[9]

When we speak of the link between shaman dancing and dervish ritual, it is interesting to note Fernand Grenard's observation of a whirling dance performed by mendicants near Tibet resembling the dancing of dervishes in every respect except one — the Tibetan dancers covered their faces with masks. The resemblance was so striking that Grénard's Moslem servants got

excited and started beating the rhy ım by clapping their hands and howling "Ya Allah! Inchah Allah!"[10] A foreign observer describes the Kalender dervishes of Khotan (Southern Tibet) in the following manner:

> The medresse Hazret Sultan... Kalendars or dervishes who resemble in some respects the Hindu fakirs and Buddhist monks...their religious dances, of which the jingling of rings on a pair of wands, or, in one case, on a goat's horn, formed a part. Also two of them sang a dervish's song holding in one hand the jingling instrument, and placing the thumb of the other under the ear, and howling with all their might.[11]

Various scholars have tried to establish parallels between the old Asiatic beliefs and practices and those of the dervish orders.[12] From these studies we understand how shamanism left its mark on dervish orders and Islam's cultural influence transformed the shaman into a Sufi. The characteristic attitudes and goals of the dervish orders preserve the memory of the Asiatic shaman — both achieve a state of trance through dancing. Additional analogies can be drawn between shamanism and the Bektaşi and village Alevi; unveiled women participated in the formal worship, and the dancing was done in couples. A Russian scholar mentions that in Eastern Turkestan there were also dances performed by couples, men and women, during shamanistic ceremonies.[13]

Except in the case of some sects and sub-sects, the rituals were open to public view — an aspect which helped to disarm the orthodox Moslem. The Mevlevi, known in Europe as "The Whirling Dervishes," and the Rufai attracted the greatest attention. Their rituals were the most sought after. Their dancing can be considered a public spectacle and exhibition. Old guide books of Istanbul and some travel accounts even indicate the days and locations of their performances and the entrance fee. For instance, in one of the French guides it is shown that the entrance fee to a *tekke* was three-quarters of a *Mecidiye* (since one *Mecidiye* was equivalent to fr. 4.25, that makes the fee approximately fr. 3.20).[14]

An interesting 16th-Century miniature (p.49) depicting the 1582 festival in Istanbul shows the Sultan watching a dervish whirling next to a dancing boy in the old Byzantine Hippodrome, each with his own musical accompaniment. Obviously, the Mevlevi dervish did not seem to mind at all performing in the open air before a vast audience of more than ten thousand, or performing next to a dancing boy, a member of a profession reputed to have unsavory connotations, including extreme lasciviousness. Another miniature depicting the same festival is rather puzzling since it shows amidst several grotesque dancers (some masked), buffoons and jesters, a figure dancing on stilts. The puzzling part is that his turban and long coat are drawn exactly like those of the Mevlevi dervish in the first miniature. He may be a real Mevlevi dervish doing a dance on stilts, since dancing on stilts was popular among the Ottomans, or he may be a buffoon dressed as a dervish trying to imitate a Mevlevi.

In public festivals not only the Mevlevi dervishes, but also other orders, performed their sacred dancing. For instance, an eyewitness of the same 1582 festival describes the participation and public display of some unorthodox wandering dervishes in the following manner:

> The Monkes followed after them, with a company of poore pilgrimes, which goe in pilgrimate to Mecque as they call it, which is the Sepulchre of Mahomet, they are counted verie holie men in Turkie: cloathed lyke Scholers, which doo nothing but labour and trotte up and downe with theyr bodies, making themselves leane, as in the ende, they loose all theyr witte and understanding: and because they rested, nor stayed not in any one place at any time, but alwayes were skipping, and dauncing about: a man might verie well compare them unto Curetes and Corybantes, the auncient Priests of Cybele, the graund mother of the two Paganes: unto them it was among all other, that Amurathe caused many small presents to be made.[15]

Many authors tend to interpret the dancing of the dervishes by the planetary system. For instance, one makes the following remark:

> We might connect the dance of the dervishes who, eight in number, move round in an orbit, though in a contrary direction, perhaps in accordance with a Mohammedan precept. In these dervishes and their dance...we may

see a survival of the mystic Cabiri, 'the Seven Great Ones,' or planetary gods, revolving round the green centre of the terrestial globe.[16]

Another sharing this opinion comments:

This, the Dervishes hold, expresses the harmony of God's creation, in an ecstasy of spiritual love, of communion with the Eternal.[17]

Another writer comments on the belt worn by some of the dervishes called the *Kamberiye* (the belt is worn in memory of Kamber, Ali's groom):

...the three stars of Orion's belt, denoting the seasons of the year...appear again in the girdle of three strands of Munja grass which every Brahmin at his initiation ties around his waist with three knots, saying as he does, that they represent the three stars on Orion's belt, the three seasons of the year; and these three stars are called in Teutonic mythology Frigg-jar rochr, the belt of Frigga, wife of Wodan the supreme god. This three-knotted girdle, called the Kamberiah, is worn by all sects of Dervishes in South-Western Asia, who are the modern representatives of the ancient dancing priests.[18]

Studying the symbolism of the Buddhist prayer wheel and its circular movement, still another writer finds a similarity between it and the whirling of the dervishes. The Brahman is supposed to reach heaven by being turned on a wheel; heaven comes down to the whirling dervishes who turn about like a wheel.[19] Still another writer mentions that, in the ritual turns and contortions of the dervishes which presumably repeat the movements of planets, are invocations and propitiations of the souls of good and evil stars, and he draws an analogy between these whirlings and the devil dances of Southern India, where malignant spirits (supposed to cause disease) are tempted into the dancers, as in a dance performed on the Island of Ceylon by three men who impersonated the forms and phases of typhus fever.[20]

Before giving a description of the Mevlevi rituals we must explain the significance of two important concepts: *sema* and *zikr*. *Sema*, in Sufism, means the listening to music, singing and chanting to attain a state of religious emotion and ecstasy (*vecd*). *Zikr* is the remembrance of Gòd by the repeated enunciation of short invocations in unison. These recitations involve regulated rhythmic breathing and physical movements for the attainment of spiritual effect. They are often accompanied by and coordinated with vocal and sometimes instrumental music which frees the physical effort from conscious thought. Both thought and will must be suspended if ecstasy is to be achieved. The *zikr* has two forms, individual and collective. Dance is an outcome of ecstasy (*vecd*), caused by the *sema*. It involves a loss of consciousness due to excessive ecstasy. Being overpowered by divine love and the *zikr*, a dervish becomes unconscious and moves the limbs of his body according to the rhythms of the tune. Sufis claim their dancing to be the work of God manifesting itself through their bodies.

The *zikr* can be divided into two kinds, one being *zikr hafî* which is the personal recollection done mentally by rhythmic breathing, and the other, *zikr cehrî* which is recollection done aloud, vocally. The latter can be done either seated (*kuudî*) or standing (*kıyamî*). The *kıyamî* can be done as the *devranî*, performed in a circle, and called *devran zikri*. All these various forms of ceremony are collectively called *mukabele-i şerife*. In some *zikr*, the dervishes subside to the ground cross-legged and later they all rise and stand. But among the Nakşibendi, the *zikr* is done seated throughout in a circle on the floor, simply by rocking backwards and forwards. And in the Halvetis' *kuud zikri* the seated adepts first ejaculate to both sides, and then kneeling they bend forward and straighten up. Of course *kıyamî zikr* is more akin to dancing.

In one form of *kıyamî zikr* called *beyyumi halaka zikri* (*halaka* means either a circle around a spiritual leader or a circle of *zikr* devotees),[21] the dervishes form a circle, each holding his neighbor on his right by his waist with his right hand, and his neighbor on his left with his left hand. In this fashion they all move round to the left. A second form is the *demdeme zikri* in which one dervish bends his body forward and backward, and his neighbor bends backward and forward and so on alternately, till at the end of the *zikr* they start to sway their bodies from side to side. Another *zikr* is called *bedevi topu*, in which a large group of dervishes encircle their sheikh and, holding each other tightly, they begin jumping. There is a *zikr* called *tavaf tevhidi* (i.e., going round for the unity of God) which has two variations. In the first, the dervishes form two facing rows. They alternately strike the floor with their feet, the two lines advancing and retreating. In some orders such as the Halveti, the two lines transform themselves into a *bedevi topu* by revolving. In the second type of *tavaf tevhidi*, dervishes either form a circle and tap the floor with their feet, or form small groups of three: each dervish places his right arm on his neighbor's waist, and his left arm on his other neighbor's shoulder, and revolves, occasionally tapping the floor with his right foot. A last example of

A 19th century posed photograph taken in the tekke.

the *kıyamî zikr* is the *vefa devri* in which the dervishes holding each other by the hand move to the left, make a line, stand close pressing their shoulders against each other, and then freeing their hands, they start backward and forward inclinations.

Sometimes, when achieving excessive ecstasy, a dervish experiences great inner power and enthusiasm, he may disengage himself from the circle, and pressing his crossed arm against his breast, whirls faster and faster until compelled by sheer exhaustion to desist. Sometimes he is so exalted that, to make him desist at a sign from the sheikh, the *meydancı dede*, who whirls with him for a while whispering God's name into his left ear, slowly makes him sit by the *mihrab* (niche in the wall of a *tekke* indicating the direction of prayer), and covers him with his garment. In the Gülşeni Order the *zikr* is carried out first during the *zikr* ejaculations which are done arm to arm; later each dervish grasps the garment of his neighbor, and the ejaculations get faster and faster.

In some orders the *zikr* is accompanied by percussion instruments such as the *kudüm* (a small single or double drum played either with a leather belt or sticks), the *mazhar* (a tambourine-like instrument), and the *halile* (cymbal). The

Mevlevi have a more elaborate orchestra, including wind and string instruments in addition to the percussion.

Some movements and formations resemble those of other orders, with slight variations. For instance, some Kadiri dervishes whirl like the Mevlevi, but without outstretching their arms. This whirling is done by one or two dervishes inside a circle, or sometimes in front of the *mihrab*. In a Halveti sub-order they first whirl individually, after which they form a circle, and later they link their arms and move to the right. The Kadiri make a circle holding each other by the hand. While revolving they increase the tempo, each placing his right arm on the right shoulder of his neighbor on his right, and his left arm on the waist of his left neighbor, making a tight formation. The Kadiri, too, form a double concentric *halaka*, the inner circle having the sheikh in its center. They do all their movements on their toes which must not leave the ground.

Some orders have elaborate and complex ceremonies, consisting of different sections like a suite; usually a slow motion is followed by a faster one. For instance, the Saadi Order practices nearly all the *zikr* of other orders including the Mevlevi, making a suite of them by arranging the different *zikr* formations of which some examples are given above.

The rituals of the Rufai Order, known among European travellers as the "howling dervishes," are divided into five distinct ceremonies, comprising

almost all those of the other orders. The dancers start by swaying themselves from side to side throwing their heads from shoulder to shoulder and placing their hands on various parts of their bodies (their faces, breasts, bellies, knees, etc.). In the second stage they move their bodies forward and backward, then from side to side, and then again back and forth. Sometimes they make two concentric circles and the more enthusiastic ones take the inner circle. Their elbows are held against each other and they observe an exact rhythm. Later they shake themselves with jerking motions and as a next step they take off their turbans, form a circle arm in arm with shoulders pressed against each other, and go round the hall at a measured pace, alternately thumping their feet on the floor in unison and springing up. Unlike the Mevlevi they are an order of self-castigation: they lick fire and pierce themselves when they attain a high state of frenzy.

The Mevlevi Order was founded in Konya by the great Turkish poet and mystic Mevlana Celaleddin Rumi. Konya, located in Central Anatolia, was the capital of the Seljuk Turks. The *devr* of the Mevlevi took its name *Devre-i Velediyye*, from Mevlana's son, Sultan Veled. Their ceremony has often been described by foreign observers. An account dated 1613 describes a visit to a "Colledge of Turkish Monkes in Galata, that are called Darvises," where, after

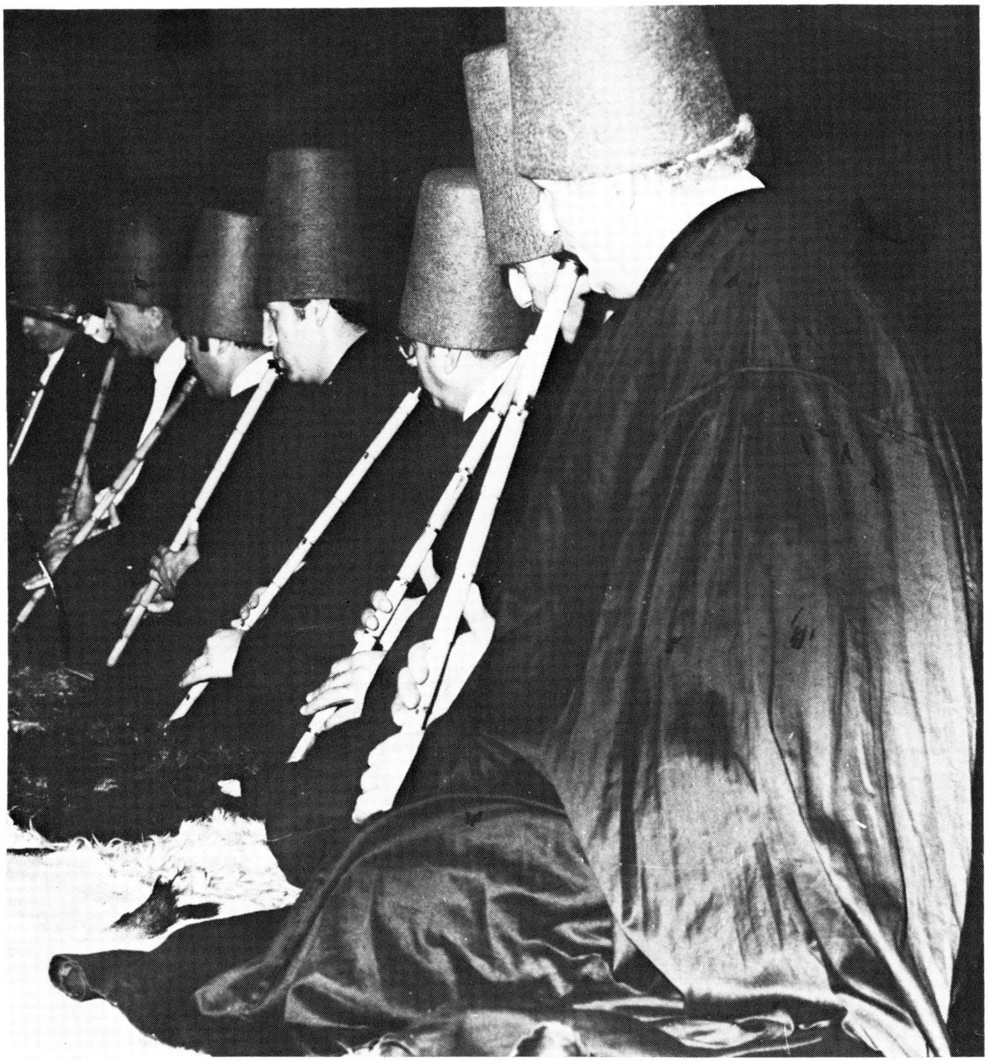

listening to much unpleasant and harsh singing and reading of the Mohemmedan law, a gentleman viewed a ceremony

> like those Trietericall Orgia that were performed by the furious Myrmalores the Priest of Bacchus. Some five and twentie of the two and fiftie Darvises, suddainly rose up bare-legged and bare-footed, and casting aside their upper Garment some of them having their brests all uncovered, they began by little and little to turne about the Interpreter of the Law, turning gently in the middest of them all, afterward they redoubled their force and turned with such incredible swiftnesse, that I could not chuse but admire it. The forme of their dauncing is as strange as the continuance of their swiftnesse, for sometimes they stretch out their Armes as far as they can in length, sometimes they contract them in a lesser compasse, sometimes they hold them about their Heads, sometimes againe they performe certaine mery gestures, as if they were drawing a Bow and shooting forth an Arrow. Likewise some of them did continue turning during the whole time in one and the selfe same place, and others move forward from one corner to another.[22]

Here is a short modern description of Mevlevi dancing: It begins with dervishes making obeisance to their leader and receiving a blessing from him. At the start their arms are crossed and pressed against their breasts with their hands grasping their shoulders and their heads inclined. Their bare feet are close together. At first they turn very slowly, their hands leaving their shoulders, and gradually the arms of the dancers are extended full length and held horizontally. Sometimes the right hand is raised with the palm turned upwards, and the left lowered with the palm turned downwards. This posture is explained symbolically by saying that the influence from heaven, received by the upturned palm, is handed down to the world below by the other. Sometimes one arm is outstretched and the other pressed against the heart. The dervishes pirouette by resting alternately on the heel of each foot while the other maintains a rotary motion. Their eyes are downcast or closed and the head is slightly bent over one shoulder. As they gradually quicken their rotation, their long white skirts become fully expanded like open umbrellas. The *semazenbaşı*, the leader of the ritual, retains his cloak and does not join the *devr*. He gives a signal for its termination and the dancers all stop at the same time. Generally there are pauses between each *devr*. Their number is symbolic of the cyclic sequence of the seasons. The whirling itself symbolizes the celestial motions; as the earth turns on its axis as well as revolving round the sun, so the dervishes pivot on their feet while making a revolution of the hall, which is considered the hall of celestial sound. The education of the Mevlevi novitiate is very arduous and painstaking; it is called the "1001 days of penitence". The preparatory exercise for whirling consists mainly of adjusting the opening of two toes around a nail on the ground and spinning around this pivot. These nails are on display in Konya.

Mevlana said: "The *sema* is the soul's adornment which helps it to discover love, to feel the shudder of the encounter, to take off the veils, and to be in the presence of God."

Even in Mevlana's time the *sema* was a spiritual discipline intended to link the Mevlevi's mind to the Infinite, leading to an emotional relationship between man and God. During Mevlana's lifetime the *sema* was not as elaborately organized as it was later to become. It was done at any time or any place, even without music. One of the source books on Mevlana states that, while wholly absorbed by his passion for God, Mevlana happened to be walking by a goldsmith's shop, and the rhythm of the pounding hammer exerted such an overwhelming influence on him that he began to whirl in ecstasy, and he made the goldsmith join him. It is said that this marked the beginning of the *sema*.

"Dancing," wrote Mevlana, "is not rising to your feet painlessly like a speck of dust blown around in the wind. Dancing is when you rise above both worlds, tearing your heart to pieces and giving up your soul."

The Mevlevi ceremony gradually evolved and grew to perfection. It integrated poetry, music (instrumental and vocal), and dancing to aid the devotee in his spiritual elevation. Its fusion of arts has continued through the centuries. Its whirling ritual, which has the attributes of a ballet performance, has inspired many European and American choreographers.

On dancing as an outcome of ecstasy prompted by the *sema*, Mevlana said:

> Dance where you can break yourself to pieces and totally abandon your worldly passions. Real men dance and whirl on the battlefield; they dance in their own blood. When they give themselves up, they clap their hands, when they leave behind the imperfections of the self, they dance. Their minstrels play music from within; and whole oceans of passion foam on the crest of their waves.

The attire of the Mevlevi dervishes who take part in the ceremony consists

of a cloak called the *cübbe* and a long white robe, the *tennure*, which is worn over a short, tight-fitting jacket, left open in front. The cylindrical, conical-shaped hat is called a *sikke*. The leaders, or high ranking dervishes, wear a turban, *destar*, around the *sikke*. The girdles are known as *eliflament*s. The area in which the ceremony is performed, the *semahane* or ritual dancing hall, is usually octagonal in form. At the opposite end from the entrance is the *mihrab*, a niche in the wall indicating the *kıble,* the direction of Mecca which Moslems face when they pray. It symbolizes the orientation of the body, the mind and the heart towards God, in short, the direction of prayer. The *minber*, as in mosques, at the top of a movable set of stairs, is the pulpit from which the preacher speaks.

A red-dyed sheepskin mat (*post*) is placed in front of and near the *mihrab*. This is the appointed seat where the leader or the sheikh of the order sits. The red color symbolizes the color of the sky at sunset, to honor Şemsüddin of Tabriz, who represents the sun. It also symbolizes Mevlana's death, and is the color of union and ceremony.

The musical performers are seated opposite the *mihrab*. The orchestra consists of the *ney* (the reed flute), the *kudüm* (a small, double kettledrum with the copper cup covered in camel or sheepskin, and played with a pair of sticks called *zahme*), the *rebab* (rebeck), originally a Turkish instrument called the *iklig* (a stringed instrument somewhat like a fiddle), and occasionally a *kanun* (a zither-like instrument with 72 strings), the *tambur* (a kind of lute), and the *ut* (another lute-like instrument).

The *semahane* is divided into two symmetrical halves starting from the *post* and extending to the entrance by an imaginary line, the *hatt-ı istiva*, meaning equator. This line, which must never be stepped on by the dervishes, represents the shortest path to God's reality and unity.

The ceremony is divided into two distinct parts. The first starts with a prayer, sometimes recitations of verses from the *Mesnevi*, followed by the *naat* or *"Naat-ı Şerif,"* a hymn in a litanic style. Although there are several *naat*s in the Mevlevi ceremony, it is customary to sing the *naat* composed by the great classical Turkish composer, Mustafa Itri (d. 1712). During this, no response is expected, there is complete silence and most of the people close their eyes. After the *naat*, the *kudümzenbaşı*, the chief double-drum player, plays four notes as a signal, and either the chief reed-piper or one of the flautists appointed by him plays a *taksim*, which is an instrumental improvisation, a kind of cadenza in the various appropriate modes, ending with the mode chosen for that day. It stimulates the first step toward an emotional uplift among the participants.

This is followed by another instrumental piece, the peşrev or prelude, which can also be played in conclusion. While the *peşrev,* which is in a 14/4 rhythm called *devr-i kebir* (grand cycle) is being played, the dervishes stand up and, headed by the sheikh, begin to march around the hall step by step, slowly and deliberately, encircling the area three times, counterclockwise.

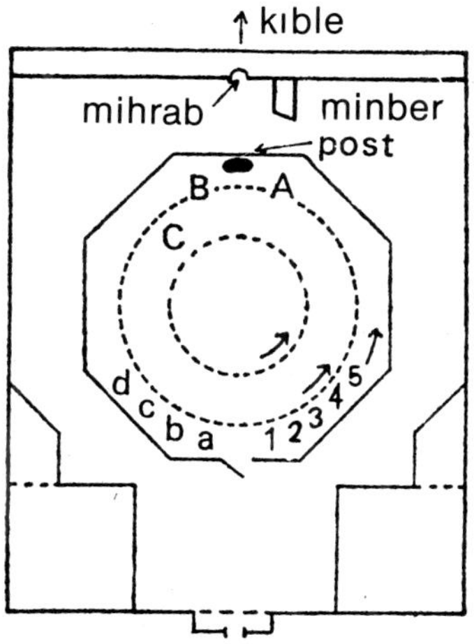

During this segment of the ritual, the dervishes salute each other in front of the *post.* Then the sheikh stands up and takes his place on the left side of the *post* (A), he bows, and walks to point (B) which is on the right side of the *post* by crossing the equator. His walk to the tempo of the *peşrev* is carried out by first stepping on the right foot, with the left slightly raised on the toes, then following a short pause, the left foot steps forward with the right slightly raised on the toes. He then presses his feet together (called *ayak mühürlemek*) by standing with the big toe of the right foot placed over the big toe of the left foot. His follower, the chief *semazen* or master of dance, who is behind him takes his place at (A), they bow their heads and each one of his followers makes the same tour and the same motions.

This ritual is repeated three times. The third time the sheikh takes his place on the *post*, and the *peşrev* music ends. This first part of the ceremony is concluded by another *ney* improvisation.

The second part of the ceremony is called the "Four *Selam*s" (*selam* is a form of salutation wishing peace, health and greeting), but in fact there are four sections of the *sema* with a *selam* for the first three only.

At the end of the fourth part, the oral segment concludes with instrumental music, i.e., *peşrev*, followed by a *yürük semai* in the 6/4 rhythmic pattern.

After the music, the dancing which we shall describe below continues till one of the singers recites from the Koran and the dancers sit down and put on their outer garments. Following this recitation, the chief *semazen* stands up and begins to pray in front of his sheikh. This supplication called the *dua-gû duası*, like the initial *post duası*, is dedicated to Mevlana and all the holy people and saints.

At the beginning of the second, or main part of the ritual, the sheikh takes

4
3

W. Hogarth
c. 1750

his station on the *post.* With the exception of the chief *semazen* and the sheikh, the dervishes lay aside their outer cloaks, leaving their undergarments and *tennures*. The chief *semazen* kisses the sheikh's hand, and the sheikh in turn kisses his. This means the sheikh gives his authorization and blessing for the *sema*, and the chief *semazen* takes his place at (C), and the other dervishes do likewise.

After kissing the sheikh's right hand and bowing, the dervishes start to whirl, each inclining his head over one shoulder, with arms crossed and hands clasped to each shoulder. As the speed increases, the arms are raised to a virtually horizontal position.

They perform a double feat of whirling and moving forward, counter-clockwise, and at the same time keeping clear of each other, maintaining their places with the regularity of clockwork. The twirling is done by pivoting on the left foot, which is called the *direk* (rod), with the right foot crossing over the top of the left instep after the manner of a paddle to keep up the motion. If a dervish keeps a fixed and stationary position, this is referred to as *direk tutmak*.

At the signal from the chief *semazen*, some dervishes whirl in the outer orbit, the others in the inner one. They repeat this three times, each time bowing to the sheikh. Kissing the hand of the sheikh is only done in the first stage of *selam*, after the salutation which involves bowing slightly, with feet pressed together, the right hand on the heart, and fingers apart.

The fourth and final period is different because the chief *semazen* does not admit anybody to the inner circle, in this period the sheikh himself takes part in the *sema*. The sheikh whirls to the center both of the equator and the hall, a point called the *kutb*. This is the place of Mevlana and his followers by succession, and the sheikh is entitled by succession to take Mevlana's place. The sheikh's whirling is slow and is called *post sema'ı*. During this phase the *ney*'s improvisation, the sound of the dancers' feet, and the rustling of their skirts make a unique harmony. While the sheikh spins back to the *post*, the *ney*'s improvisation and the whole *sema* end abruptly.

As in most other Sufi rituals, the Mevlevi ceremonies are full of symbolism. A small manuscript of the 15th Century (there are two copies extant: in Istanbul's Fatih Library, No. 5335; and in Ankara's Halk Library, No. 320), is probably the first complete treatise on dancing in Turkey. It reinforces, with literary proof, the views and theories which we had already formed from a study of the dances themselves. The unknown author of the old manuscript traces the development of dance from its spiritual brith at the creation of the world. He states that when God created the universe, divine energy resounded and from that sound arose the twelve tonalities of music, and this gave birth to four different types of dancing, *çarh, raks, muallak* and *pertav*. Out of this creation emerged a Sufi dressed in blue (*sofi-i ezrak pûş*) who started whirling.

Çarh is a Persian word meaning "wheel" or "revolving object," and the dances of this group are of a whirling and circling nature. *Raks*, generally meaning "dance," in this context is used to mean more specifically the movements of the arms, hands, legs and head with the torso of the body remaining static. *Muallak,* in Arabic meaning "hanging object," denotes leaping and jumping, which are classified as the vertical movements; and *pertav,* also a Persian word meaning "physical forward projection," covers the group of dances with horizontal movement.

The author goes on to link the physical movement of the body in dance with the spiritual experience of the dance itself. It is here that he mentions the

Emilyan Mihailoviç Korneyev (1780-1839)

word *sema*. The connotations of this word are interesting, for its meaning is twofold. In the first place, the word means "listening to music" but, with a different spelling, it has another meaning, namely "the heavens". It is obvious how the idea of listening, dancing and spiritual experience became intermingled. Indeed the religious side of people's life was closely linked to dance, for the religious leader and the leader of the dance *sema* were the same person. The room in which this dance was performed symbolized the year, the leader himself represented the sun, the life-giver of the earth, and the dancers revolved around him like the stars and moon in the *çarh*, *raks*, *muallak* and *pertav*. These symbolized the four seasons, which are born of the twelve months, represented, no doubt, by the twelve tonalities of music from which the four dances evolved. The circling movements of the *çarh* symbolized the evolution of winter into spring and characterized the rebirth of the earth in springtime. The limb movements of the *raks* represented the tranquility and life-giving qualities of summer, the movements themselves bearing a close resemblance and affinity to the movements of leaves and petals. The *muallak* depicted autumn, its leaping vertical movements expressing the feelings of heavy ripeness, maturity and thanksgiving to be found in this season. The *pertav* represented winter — its forward movements symbolizing the fallen leaves, the dead flowers, the drooping trees and the barreness of the season.

The four dances, too, were linked not only to the four seasons but also to the four elements. When the dances were performed, there was a relationship between inner spiritual ecstasy and physical movement. This relationship

gave symbolic roots to the relationship of the dance and the four elements of which the human body was said to be comprised.

We have no room to comment on all the symbolism of this manuscript, only on the essential points. From the foregoing summary we can conclude that the whole cosmos is a dancing mystery, and mysticism recognized dancing as a symbol of the cosmos. All the creatures carry out their function in the way fixed by and through the power of the leader (the Sufi clad in blue) who represents God. They are, therefore, interdependent, because he would not be able to realize his power without them.

Mevlana articulated how, during the dance, the *semazen* senses in himself the movements of the stars:

Each atom dancing in the plain
Or on the air
Behold it well, like us, insane
It spinneth there
Each atom, whether glad it be
Or sorrowful,
Circleth the sun in ecstasy
Ineffable.

(Tr. A. J. Arberry)

In the ceremony described there are other metaphors — a Mevlevi's hat symbolizes the gravestone, his cloak his coffin, and his white tunic his shroud. The *ney* represents the mythological trumpet called the *sur*; the trumpet blast of the angel of death İsrafil wakes the dead on the Day of Resurrection.

In the axially divided *semahane*, the right half is the tangible world, the

visible world, and the left half is the invisible world, the angel's world. With the sound of the *ney*, the dead are resurrected from their tombs and attain eternal life through the guidance of the sheikh; they are the divine truth, the truth of unity.

In the *devr-i kebir* the number three is symbolic. The first orbit epitomizes knowledge of God, the knowledge of certainty; the second represents the seeing God, the eye of certainty; and the third is the stage of true existence, the truth of unity. One end of the equator where the sheikh sits is divine nature, the opposite end is human nature. This way the right semicircle stands for the descent from divine nature, from the absolute, to human nature; the left semicircle ascends from human nature. In other words, the right represents descent to material perfection, and the left ascends to spiritual perfection, to contemplative life. His body in standing position and his outstretched arms form the words *la* and *lila* in the Arabic script — representing the unity of God.

On December 17, 1273 A.D., the poet Mevlana Celaleddin Rumi, founder of the Mevlevi Sufi brotherhood, died in Konya. He was a philosopher and mystic of Islam, but not a Moslem of the orthodox type. His doctrine advocates unlimited tolerance, positive reasoning, goodness, charity, and awareness through love. To him and to his disciples all religions are more or less truth. Looking with the same eye on Moslem, Jew and Christian alike, his peaceful and tolerant teaching has appealed to men of all sects and creeds. Mevlana was laid to rest beside his father and over his remains, a splendid shrine was erected. The 13th-Century Mevlana Mausoleum with its mosque, dance hall, dervish living quarters, school, and tombs of some of the leaders of the Mevlevi Order continues to this day to draw pilgrims from all parts of the Moslem and non-Moslem world.

The Mevlana annual festival is held every year in Konya starting at the beginning of December. It lasts two weeks and its culminating point is the *Şeb-i Arus,* (Nuptial Night), December 17. The night of Mevlana's death is thus called because of the union of Mevlana with God. This festival attracts crowds of every race,color and creed from all around the world. It is very different from many other periodic commemorations of venerated saints: It provides a unique opportunity for outsiders to witness this esoteric rite, a visual manifestation of Sufi mysticism in its own setting. Also, this rite is the means of having communion of love with God, drawing man nearer to the Almighty, stimulating concurrently an emotional approach to reality and an emotional attachment to God. It is not an ordinary pilgrimage, as Mevlana's epitaph states:

When we are dead, seek not our tomb in
the earth, but find it in the hearts of men.

During the Ottoman Empire the numerous Sufi dervish orders exerted widespread influence. There were strong rivalries between these orders whose numbers have been estimated up to 140 or more. The Mevlevi Order, centralized in Anatolia, had a few branches in Damascus, Aleppo, Tripoli, and important branches in the European regions of the Empire, especially in Salonika. As the Bektaşi were more rural in character, their supporters were concentrated in the villages, while the Mevlevi fraternity, urban, sophisticated and more centralized, was supported by intellectuals and the government circles and thus attracted greater attention. Many great Turkish composers such as Mustafa Dede (1610-1675), Mustafa Itri (1640-1711), İsmail Dede (1777-

1845), the Ottoman Sultan Selim III (1761-1808) and others contributed great and inspired musical compositions to the Mevlevi ceremony.

The dervish orders began playing a political role during the constitutional period in Turkey starting in 1908. On December 13, 1925, a law was passed closing all the *tekke*s (dervish lodges), *zaviye*s (central dervish lodges), and shrines and other places of pilgrimage (*ziyaret*). Istanbul alone had more than 250 *tekke*s as well as small centers for the meetings of various fraternities. This law dissolved the orders, prohibited the use of mystical names, titles, and costumes pertaining to such titles, impounded their assets, and banned their ceremonies and meetings. It also provided sentences for those who tried to re-establish them. Two years later, in 1927, the Mausoleum of Mevlana in Konya was allowed to reopen as a museum. Another change occurred much later in 1953 when the present annual ceremony of Mevlana was revived and an audience was invited to a movie theater in Konya for a first authorized Mevlevi ceremony (although ceremonies were still held privately and secretly). After Turkey's adoption of the multi-party democratic system, this was a government concession to religious revival and a safety valve to resolve the tension between the ardent Moslem people and their Westernized leaders.

December 17, 1954 was the 681st anniversary of the death of Mevlana, and the following year permission was granted for a public ceremony again in a movie theater. In 1956, the ceremony was performed in the library in Konya, and in the same year a parallel ceremony was organized in Ankara. As the ceremonies drew larger crowds they were transferred to a large auditorium in Konya, and ever since there has been an annual performance in Konya in the month of December. In 1973 the government authorized performances to be given in London, Paris and in the U.S.A., to mark the 700th anniversary of the death of Mevlana.

The Mevlevi Order, perhaps the most distinguished order and the best known in Europe, with an intellectual appeal, is free from extravagances and its dance is not accompanied by self-castigation as practiced by some other orders. Mevlevi dancing is almost like a ballet performance, and has inspired many dancers in the West. For instance, on April 9, 1761, a performance of the play *Soliman the Second* by C. S. Favart, contained a divertissement inspired by the Whirling Dervishes; and on December 20, 1788, at the Paris Théatre du Grands Danseurs du Roi a ballet was performed called *Les Derviches* which was also based on the Mevlevi ritual. The Ballet Suédois on November 13, 1920, premiered a Mevlevi-inspired ballet called *Dervishes*, with choreography by Jean Borlin to Alexander Glazounov's music and with a setting designed by Mouveau which represented a Mevlevi *tekke*. Some individual dancers, too, were inspired — the American Ted Shawn who presented his *Mevlevi Dervish* and the German Dore Hoyer who did *Drehtanz*.

The above examples are mere attempts to explain Whirling Dervish rituals in terms of pure dance movements or as manifestations of Eastern mysticism and exoticisim. However, today, important theater directors in the Western world look to the Eastern rituals, particularly to the Sufi dervish rituals, as a most potent source of artistic inspiration for the modern stage. A prominent pioneer of this movement is the Caucasian-born Russian mystic George Ivanovich Gurdjieff whose esoteric teaching has found adherents among directors, choreographers, musicians, designers, painters, writers and psychologists like Nikolai Evreinov, Serge Diaghilev, Thomas de Hartmann, Alexander and Jeanne Salzmann, Louis Jouvet, Felix Labisse, J. B. Priestley, Aldous Huxley, Katherine Mansfield, Frank Lloyd Wright, Moshe Feldenkrais, Peter Brook, *et al.* To create his school of thought, Gurdjieff drew

on pre-Christian Assyrian, devil-worshipping Yezidi, Phrygian, Zoroastrian, Tibetan, and Sufi rituals, and particularly on the Whirling Dervishes. In 1920 Gurdjieff led his Institute into exile in Turkey, and studied the techniques of the Rufai and Mevlevi rituals during the intermittent performances staged in Istanbul. Later his troupe travelled across Europe and in the U.S.A., always incorporating some elements of the Whirling Dervish movements combined with other dervish dancing from Central Asia, Christian Assyrian ritual, and folk and country dances from Turkey and Transcaspia. The male members of his company were generally attired exactly like the Whirling Dervishes.

Richard Schechner, founder and Co-director of the Performance Group and Professor of Drama at New York University, believes that any ritual can be lifted from its original setting and performed as theater. After watching a performance of the Whirling Dervishes of Konya in 1972 at the Brooklyn Academy of Music he wrote:

> Part one of the program was selected instrumental dervish compositions and improvisations played by the Chamber ensemble. Then a fifteen minute intermission. Then The Ceremony of the Mevlevi, which the program tells us is performed every year in Konya, December 2 - 17..... The ceremony concludes with an intonation of the mystical word for The One "Huuuuuu....u....u...u". I won't describe the performance, except to say that it was extraordinarily moving and simple. I know that several theatre groups in New York were influenced by it. Within the last year Robert Wilson, at least three dance companies, and the Performance Group have used dervish whirling either in workshops or in public performances.

Robert Wilson, whose name is mentioned in the above quotation, one of the theater geniuses of our time, is almost obsessed by the Whirling Dervishes. In many performances, his company, the Byrr Hoffman Group, has used Mevlevi whirling movements. Andy Degroat, the leading dancer and choreographer of the Wilson group, was the first to begin the whirling. In Robert Wilson's *Ka Mountain and Gardenia Terrace*, set amid the ruins of Persepolis and the mountains near Shiraz, the Whirling Dervish dance figures prominently in one episode. The performances lasted seven days, a total of 168 hours. In another work by Wilson called *The Life and Times of Joseph Stalin*, the whirling dance is the most important element in the fifth act entitled "The Temple " in which Andy Degroat spun for about forty minutes non-stop and at moments was joined by other members of the company. The performance, divided into seven acts, started at 7 p.m. and continued until 7 a.m. In Wilson's *Einstein on the Beach*, the performers, attired in gray, brown or white, walk slowly on stage one by one, the way the Whirling Dervishes make their entrance. In his *Letter for Queen Victoria*, two dancers whirl continuously on stage. And lastly in Wilson's *The Dollar Value of Man*, there is a sequence where performers whirl for ten minutes. In the seventh scene of the same work, this whirling is repeated. In almost all of Wilson's work, number seven holds a prominent place which is probably another Sufi influence, since the number seven is a symbolically significant number among the Sufis.

Alongside the cultural impact of Mevlana's verses, paeans to love, and humanistic Sufism, the ritual whirling of his Mevlevi sect continues to exert wide influence outside the realm of Islam.

NOTES

Notes for "Love Is All: Mevlana's Poetry and Philosophy"

1) His coffin is in the city of Konya not far from the Mevlana Mausoleum-Museum.

2) Turkish titles for these works are *Divan-ı Şems-i Tebriz* and *Divan-ı Kebir* respectively.

3) Ironically very few surveys of humanism, of world literature, or histories of civilization so much as cite Mevlana's name. His poetry is included in very few anthologies of world poetry. Most encyclopaedias give him only cursory comments or a few paragraphs at best.

The fault lies partly with Middle Eastern scholars themselves. They have long been suffering from an acute feeling of inferiority about their own culture, religious or national. They have over-admired and over-acquired the cultural norms and values of the West to the denigration of their own indigenous heritage. Those who are tradition-bound often remain reactionary. Yet, few have effectively interpreted the philosophy, the arts, and the poetry of the Middle East for the benefit of the world. Anthologies of world literature and histories of the world will, consequently, underplay or sometimes by-pass the Moslem world. Mevlana is a victim of the same phenomenon.

Part of the reason, however, is that Mevlana's poetry has not been fortunate enough to have translators of the calibre of Edward FitzGerald, whose translation of Omar Khayyam is perhaps the best-known example of Persian poetry in the West. Mevlana's English translators are "19th-Century gentlemen" chronologically or aesthetically: well-meaning, diligent, often meticulous poetasters who could find rhymes, strait jacket lines into meters, and squeeze all life out of poetry. In their hands, adept at archaicisms and exoticisms, a great disservice has been perpetrated against Mevlana's poetry. Even his best translator, Reynold A. Nicholson, could write such monstrosities as "If so be that thou throwest a glance upon (aught in) the two worlds, do not so," which was bad style even in the 19th Century. As recently as 1956, Sir Colin Garbett published such gems as "Yestreen unto a star I cried / To thee my words I trust" and "Forth shalt thou tread / And thy two feet shalt shed." A highly respected scholar of Arabic and Persian literatures, A. J. Arberry, also tried his hand at translation. Among his versions of Mevlana's *rubaiyat*, published in 1949, there are such grotesque inversions as "His music when he played / Me clapping hands He made."

Notes for "Sema: The Spiritual Concert of the Mevlevis"

1 For various quotations and bibliographical notes from early texts see Marijan Molé, "la Danse Extatique en Islam", *Les Danses Sacrées,* Paris 1963, pp. 147-280; for four early manuscripts in Arabic on dancing, see Henry George Farmer, "The Sources of Arabian Music: An Annotated Bibliography...", *Records of the glasgow Bibliographical Society, XIII (1939).* Issued separately in 1940.

2 Duncan B. Macdonald, "Emotional Religion in Islam as affected by Music and Singing', Translation of a book of the 'Ihya 'Ulum ad-Din" of al-Ghazzali, *Journal of the Royal Society,* 1901, pp. 195-252: 705-48.

3 See Reynold Alleyne Nicholson, *Studies in Islamic Mysticism,* Cambridge 1921, p. 234, 57-58.

4 Abu 'l-Hasan Ali al-jullabi-Hujwiri, *Kashf al-mahjub,* abridged tr. R.A. Nicholson, E.J. W. Gibb Memorial volume, XVII, Leyden-London 1911, p. 416

5 In practice *fetvas,* or sentences given on a matter of Canon Law, delivered by Muftis: For a selection of fetvas concerning the theatre, see And A *History...,* p. 12.

6 On these arguments for and against, see Sirajul Haq, "Samâ and Raqs of the dervishes", *Islamic Culture: The Hyderabad Quarterly Review* (1944), pp. 111-130.

7 G.L. Lewis, *The Balance of Truth,* Translation of "Mizan ül-hakk fi ihtiyar-il-ahakk', by Kâtip Çelebi, London 1957, pp. 42-43.

8 Arminius Vambéry, *Sketches of Central Asia: Additional Chapters on My Travels, Advantures and on the Ethnology of Central Asia,* London 1868, pp. 4-5.

9 Arminius Vambéry, "Voyage dans l'Asie Centrale", *Le Tour du Monde,* Paris, XII (1865), p. 96 (illustration on page 97).

10 Fernand Grenard, *Mission Scientifique dans la Haute Asie (1890-1895)* II, p. 137, 236 ff.

11 Henry Lansdell, *Chinese Central Asia: A Ride to little Tibet,* London 1893, II, p. 195.

12 For instance see Fuat Köprülü's *Influence du Chamamisme Turco-Mongol sur les Ordres Mystiques Musulmans,* İstanbul 1929. By a strange coincidence in the same year, that is in 1929, a similar approach can be seen in a German study, see Else Krohn, "Vorislamiches in einigen vorderasiatischen Sekten und Derwiskorden", *Etnologische Studien,* Leipzig, 1/4 (1929), pp. 311-13.

13 See Sergei Oldenburg, "Short notes on Peri-Kohn and Dua-Khon in Koochara" (in Russian), *Sbornik Mouzeia Antropoplogii I Etnografii Pri Rossiskoi Akademii Nauk,* V/1 (1918, p 18. Also for couples dancing in Khotan see Ella C. Skyes and Sir Percy Sykes, *Through Deserts and Oases of Central Asia, London* 1920, p. 323.

14 See Henry Borotra, *Lettres Orientales,* Paris 1893, p. 37.

15 George Lebelski, *A True Description of the Magnificall Tryumphes and Pastimes, represented at Constantinople... in the yeare of our Lorde God 1582...* Published in François de Billerberg. *Most Rare and Strange Discourses of Amurathe, The Turkish Emperor that now is,* London 1585 [no pagination].

16 William Copeland Borlose, *The Dolmens of Ireland...,* London 1897, III, p. 739.

17 Victoria De Bunsen, *The Soul of a Turk,* London 1910, pp. 181-182.

18 J.F. Hewitt, *Primitive Traditional History,* London 1907, I. p. 158.

19 William Simpson, *The Buddhist Praying Wheel,* London 1896, pp. 137-139.

20 M. Daniel Conway, *Demonology and Devil-Lore,* London 1879, I. pp. 250-51.

21 "In the same manner as the dance of the spheres in the Samothracian mysteries has been preserved to our days in the slow circle dance of the Mevlevi's in which each der-

BIOGRAPHICAL NOTES

Metin And is one of Turkey's most prominent and prolific scholars. He is the author of more than forty books and more than a thousand articles on drama, dance, miniature painting, magic and ritual.

Dr. And studied drama in London after obtaining a degree in law at the University of Istanbul. Later he conducted research on the theater in the United States on a Rockefeller Fellowship. He holds a PhD from the University of Ankara where he is a Professor in the Department of Drama.

His books in Turkish include such major volumes as "Traditional Turkish Theater", "Turkish Theater from 1839 to 1923", "Ottoman Theater", "Turkish Theater from 1923 to 1973", "Byzantine Theater" (which is the second work ever of its kind in any language), and "Games and Magic" (one of the best studies available in any language). His study of shadow plays in Turkey and throughout the world is probably the most comprehensive study of its kind.

Dr. And has published many other works including studies of the Turk in European drama, opera and ballet, of Ottoman festivities, of Dionysus and the Anatolian peasant, and of Turkish peasant dances.

His history of the traditional Turkish theater won the coveted award of the Turkish Language Society in 1970.

Prof. And's books in English include *Dances of Anatolian Turkey, A History of Theatre and Popular Entertainment in Turkey, Turkish Miniature Painting, Karagöz: Turkish Shadow Theatre, Magic in Istanbul,* and *Turkish Dancing.*

Metin And has travelled extensively in the Middle East, Europe, Asia, and North America, giving lectures and doing research. His contributions have appeared in many books, encyclopedias, journals and collections in numerous countries.

For many years he served on the three-member dramaturgical board of the Turkish State Theaters. In the 1950s and 1970s he was a performing arts critic for some of Turkey's leading newspapers and art magazines. His programs were frequently broadcast on the Turkish radio network. He has also served as Editor of *Forum*, one of Turkey's major intellectual journals.

Prof. And has conducted extensive research about the dances of Anatolia and their origins. He has also studied the rituals of the Whirling Dervishes and other sects of Islamic mysticism.

---

vish moves round himself as a central point, and all move together round the sheikh who stands in the middle, so may we distinguish in the violent simultaneous movement backwards and forwards, and sideways, of the Rufal dervishes, the ancient... Persian dance of the Thesmaphorians. All the representations of Athanaeus and Pollux respecting them accord perfectly with the above description, The dancers sank down forwards, then raised themselves up again, representing the motion of the ox sinking and rising under its burthen." John Murray, ed. *A Handbook for Travellers in Turkey Describing Constantinople, European Turkey, Asia Minor, Armenia, and Mesopotamia.* London, 1854, pp. 120-121.

22 Samuel Purchas, *Hakluytus Posthumus or Purchas His Pilgrimes Contayning a History of the World in Sea Voyages and Lande Travells by Englishmen and others.* Reprint of 1625 edition, Glasgow, 1905, vol. X. pp. 418-19.

Talat Sait Halman is the author of numerous books and articles on the Islamic mystics of Anatolia, principally Mevlana Celaleddin Rumi and Yunus Emre. He has also lectured extensively in several countries on the Sufis. He has published three books on Yunus Emre: *The Humanist Poetry of Yunus Emre* (1972), *Yunus Emre and His Mystical Poetry* (1981, 1990, 1991), and *Selected Poems* (1990). The first has been translated into Urdu (published in Pakistan, 1975) and into Persian (published in Iran, 1976).

Himself a poet, Halman has published five collections of his original poems in Turkish. His poems in English (with their French versions by Louise Gareau-Des Bois) came out in Canada in 1979 *(Shadows of Love/Les ombres de l'amour)* and in the United States in 1990 *(A Last Lullaby).*

Other volumes published by Halman include *Contemporary Turkish Literature, Modern Turkish Drama,* and several volumes of his translations of Turkish poetry into English. His books in Turkish include translations of Shakespeare's Sonnets, selected poems of Wallace Stevens and Langston Hughes, three books relating to William Faulkner, books on Eskimo and ancient Egyptian poetry, and a major collection of the poetry of ancient civilizations.

Hundreds of scholarly articles, critical essays, reviews, encyclopedia entries, and newspaper articles he has published in several countries remain uncollected.

In 1971, he served as Turkey's Minister of Culture in a national coalition cabinet, becoming the first person to hold this post in Turkish history.

Currently a Professor of Near Eastern Languages and Literatures at New York University, he has also been on the faculties of Columbia University, Middle East Technical University, New School for Social Research, the University of Pennsylvania, and Princeton University for many years. He spent the academic year 1990-1991 at the University of Michigan on a Rockefeller Fellowship in the Humanities.

From 1980 to 1982 he served as Turkey's Ambassador for Cultural Affairs and Deputy Permanent Representative at the United Nations.

He is a member of the Poetry Society of America and American as well as Turkish PEN Center. From 1974 to 1981 he was a member of the Executive Board of the American PEN Center and represented it as an offical delegate at the International Congresses in Ohrid, Jerusalem, Paris, London, Sydney, and Stockholm.

He has served as Guest Editor for the Turkish or Near Eastern issues of several journals — *The Literary Review, The Bulletin of the Poetry Society of America, Literature East and West, Books Abroad, Pacific Quarterly, Review of National Literatures, Contemporary Literature in Translation. Literature in Translation,* and *Translation: The Journal of Literary Translation:*

His other Dost books are *Süleyman the Magnificent - Poet, The Tales of Nasrettin Hoca, Living Poets of Turkey,* and *Turkish Legends and Folk Poems.*

In 1971 he was decorated Knight Grand Cross ("The Most Excellent Order of the British Empire") by Queen Elizabeth II. His honors and awards include an honorary doctorate from Istanbul's Bosphorus University, two translation prizes, and Columbia University's "Thornton Wilder Prize". Since 1991 he has been serving as an elected member of UNESCO's Executive Council.

BOOKS BY DOST PUBLICATIONS

TURKISH MINIATURE PAINTING by Metin And

The Ottoman Period. 68 miniatures in full color and 107 black and white illustrations, 17×24, 142 p., English.

KARAGÖZ: Turkish Shadow Theatre By Metin And

98 full color and 160 Black and white illustrations 17×24, hard cover, 118 p., English.

MEVLANA CELALEDDİN RUMİ AND THE WHIRLING DERVISHES
by Talat S. Halman & Metin And

Sufi philosophy, whirling rituals, poems of ecstasy, miniature paintings. 33 full color and 30 black and white illustrations, 20×28, 112 p., English.

SÜLEYMAN THE MAGNIFICENT - POET

30 poems by Süleyman the Magnificent, translated into English with an introduction by Talat S. Halman; foreword by Esin Atıl. 11 miniatures and paintings in color, 17×24, hard cover, 88 p.

French edition: Translated by Edouard Roditi, soft cover, 84 p. (ISBN 975-7499-01-3)

THE TALES OF NASRETTİN HOCA Told by Aziz Nesin

Retold in English by Talat S. Halman, illustrations by Zeki Fındıkoğlu. 40 illustrations in full color, 17×24, 120 p. (ISBN 975-95481-0-0)

French Edition: Translated by Dominique Halbout du Tanney, 120 p. (ISBN 975-7499-04-8)

German Edition: Translated by Sybille Çizenel, 120 p. (ISBN 975-7499-06-4)

THE BLUE PARADISE OF LYCIA by Temuçin Aygen

The story of a Blue Voyage and the history of the ancient civilizations of Lycia, with color photographs and maps of ancient cities, also included a color map and chart of bays. 17×24, 120 p., English. (ISBN 975-95481-1-9)

LIVING POETS OF TURKEY

An anthology of modern poems translated into English by Talat S. Halman with an introduction on Turkish poetry. 17×24, 160 p. (ISBN 975-7499-00-5)

SELECTION OF 33 TURKISH MINIATURES

Text by Metin And. The Ottoman Period. 33 color plates, 33×47, hard cover, 72 p., English, German.

TURKISH LEGENDS AND FOLK POEMS
by Talat S. Halman

Three most beloved Anatolian tales and legends and the life stories and selected poems of four great Turkish folk poets. 28 color illustrations by Zeki Fındıkoğlu. 17×24, 110 p., English. (ISBN 975-7499-07-2)

TURKISH PAINTERS/LES PEINTRES TURCS: FIKRET MOUALLA
by Türkkaya Ataöv

Life story of the famous Turkish painter Fikret Moualla. 40 full color and 24 black and white reproductions of his works. 22×23, hard cover, 88 p., English-French. (ISBN 975-7499-08-0)

TURKISH MINIATURES ALBUM (I, II, III)

6 posters in full color, 35×50.

TURKISH CALLIGRAPHY ALBUM (V)

6 posters in full color, 35×50.

ALBUM C- 1, 2, 3, 4 (Istanbul Engravings 1840, Turkish Miniatures, Turkish Calligraphy, Miniatures of Mevlana Calaleddin Rumi) 6 posters in full color, 25×35.